ELITE

A Modern Success Guide to Purpose and Peak Performance

ELITE

A MODERN SUCCESS GUIDE TO PURPOSE AND PEAK PERFORMANCE

BRAD BELLARD, MD

ELITE

A Modern Success Guide to Purpose and Peak Performance
Published by Purposely Created Publishing Group™
Copyright © 2019 Brad Bellard

All rights reserved.

No part of this book may be reproduced, distributed or transmitted in any form by any means, graphic, electronic, or mechanical, including photocopy, recording, taping, or by any information storage or retrieval system, without permission in writing from the publisher, except in the case of reprints in the context of reviews, quotes, or references.

Printed in the United States of America

ISBN: 978-1-949134-92-6

Special discounts are available on bulk quantity purchases by book clubs, associations and special interest groups. For details email: sales@publishyourgift.com or call (888) 949-6228.
For information log on to www.PublishYourGift.com

DEDICATION

This book is for all the professionals who know there's "more in the tank" and aren't yet maximizing their full potential. For the successful professional who has goals they've consistently missed the mark on, whether professional or personal, and are tired of not getting results they want. It's also for the professional who is tired of settling, accepting average, and is ready to achieve the next level of results and success. It's for those professionals looking to maximize their performance in both their personal and professional lives. In this book, lies the keys to results and peak performance you've desired to experience.

This is also for all the professionals going after your dreams and the ones still trying to figure out what your dreams are. This is also dedicated to the successful professional who has reached a level of success they initially dreamed of, only to find that their true purpose wasn't being fulfilled once they achieved it. For the professional who has asked questions like, "Is this it?! Is there more out there for me?" In this book, lies the keys to help you discover and live that life of purpose you've yearned to live.

This book will serve as your success guide to purpose and peak performance! It's time for the best version of you to come to life!

TABLE OF CONTENTS

Preface ix

Introduction 1

1 Core Formula 3

2 Manifestation Mindset 19

3 Clear Purpose 39

4 Defined Goals 53

5 Morning Habit (Power Hour) 71

6 Consistency 85

7 Resilience 97

Epilogue 107

About the Author 109

PREFACE

I am a double-boarded emergency and sports medicine physician and former assistant team physician to the National Basketball Association (NBA) Dallas Mavericks. I am also a regular guest on the Dallas ESPN 103.3FM radio show, *Inside Sports Medicine*. I've successfully run a direct sells business with over 1,200 customers and I am currently the CEO of Bellard Enterprises and Dr. Brad MD. I am a published author, transformational keynote speaker, performance coach, husband to a beautiful wife, and father to three awesome children. However, about three years ago, despite the outward success, I was underachieving and unfulfilled. On the outside, it all looked great! But when I looked in the mirror there were two things I couldn't deny: First, contrary to what many people thought, I wasn't living up to my full potential. I was playing small. Yes, I had successfully achieved the prestigious goal of becoming a physician and I was achieving success as a direct sales business owner. However, despite this outward display of what many would define as successful, my actual performance in all areas of my life was very average—often below average—and so were my results. I was simply settling for less, going through the motions in all areas of my life, and my results reflected that. I had to face the fact that I knew I wasn't living the best version of me, and it was primarily because of mediocre effort. I was underachieving relative to the standard of performance I knew could be achieved and therefore, despite having reached a certain level of success, I had an average life with average results. That was a difficult, yet much needed pill to swallow. Second, I wasn't fulfilled. I vividly remember being at home alone preparing to work another 24hr ER shift. I was extremely busy at the time, and my stress was at an all-time high. I felt overwhelmed and dissatisfied knowing I was heading to another monotonous shift where I would be overworked, unfulfilled, and consistently have much less impact than I anticipated as a physician. I felt as if I wasn't fulfilling my real purpose. I remember thinking, "Did I make the right career decision?" In the middle of getting ready, I broke down on my knees next to the bed, tears in my eyes, my head buried in my hands, and I cried out loud, "Is this it?! God, it's just got to be better than this!" I was trying to figure out how I'd done all this work, spent all this money, put in all this effort, achieved my goal, and still didn't feel like I was living out my purpose. It didn't make sense to me. I remember thinking, "Success is not supposed to feel this way and this MUST change!"

After making the decision to change, the first thing I did was immediately reach out to the most successful and fulfilled person I knew. I knew I would need help on this journey. He'd served as a mentor and coach in my life and he lived the results that I wanted. Therefore, I knew he had answers I was looking for. I was also very willing and open to do whatever he said in order to achieve similar levels of performance and fulfillment. Three things were responsible for my transformation: (1) an understanding of the importance of my mindset and beliefs, (2) my willingness to learn from coaches and mentors and, (3) taking action. As a result, my life changed from under-achievement and lack of purpose and fulfillment, to all-time highs in goal achievement, and happiness, both professionally and personally. My transformation has allowed me to experience more success in my medical practice, discovery and pursuit of my purpose (which you are now experiencing from the publishing of this book), and increased performance in multiple areas of my life. This has resulted in the most income I've ever made, being in the absolute best health I've ever been in, a joyful marriage and family life, and the best connection with God I've ever had. The principles in this book have been nothing short of an absolute game-changer in my life and I am truly blessed because of it. So now I am here to help create the exact same transformation in you. It is my purpose and moral obligation to pay the blessing forward, to serve as your success guide to purpose and peak performance in your life.

INTRODUCTION

Elite Professional: The motivated modern-day professional who maximizes their overall performance to experience both professional success and personal fulfillment.

Dictionary.com defines the word "elite" as "A group of persons of the highest class." However, there is what I like to describe as the elite professional. They are considered "elite" because this lifestyle is certainly practiced by a 'group of *professionals* of the highest class'. This "elite" class of professional is indeed uncommon for our modern culture because they simultaneously experience both professional success *and* genuine personal fulfillment. Unfortunately, all too common in our current professional community, exists what I phrase as "the successfully unfulfilled professional", defined by successful achievement professionally, but a lack of personal happiness and fulfillment. Elite professionals intentionally aspire, to live the best version of themselves in all areas of life. They practice a lifestyle that is founded upon the idea that success, is not success at all, without accompanied fulfillment!

The purpose of this book is to serve as a guide to help today's professional community experience new levels of success, achievement, and fulfillment by maximizing their performance both personally and professionally, so they can experience a life of simultaneous purpose and peak performance.

Remember, this is a guide. This book is intended to take notes from, to reference, and take along with you. It achieves its greatest impact by reading and reviewing as much as needed until it becomes common practice. My goal is for professionals to learn and practice a way of life that achieves results in their personal and professional lives without forfeiting their happiness. This book is to help you begin turning on all cylinders of life toward living the best version of yourself, every day. It is also meant to help you understand that the life you desire doesn't happen by chance, but by intention, purpose-driven belief, and action. Elite requires a purpose-driven lifestyle that can be learned and practiced to create extraordinary results, and allow you to experience high levels of both professional success and personal fulfillment at the same time!

CORE FORMULA

Anything that is going to be built must start with a foundation. A foundation is the most important part of a structure. It provides the strength, support, and sturdiness with which what is built on top will reliably stand. With the appropriate foundation, a structure can stand strong without fear of breaking down despite whatever outside forces or challenges it may face. Take any structure—house, building, roads, bridges, vehicles, and even less tangible structures such as companies—they all start with a foundation, and the more firm and rooted the foundation, the longer they last, the more challenges they can withstand, and the more storms they can weather. Our lives are no different. We must have a firm foundation built upon principles such that when faced with challenges and adverse forces, it can withstand anything. But these firm and sturdy structures aren't built to be able to withstand strong outside forces by mere chance. Large masterpieces and iconic structures like the Golden Gate Bridge or the Eiffel Tower never just happen by chance. It happened by intention! Someone had a vision of what they wanted to create. They developed purpose-driven plans, then took action to make what they envisioned come to reality. And not only did that vision come to reality, it was built on a firm foundation, and therefore we stand in awe of its greatness and ability to last and stand strong. Again, our lives are no different! An awesome masterpiece life is very possible! That masterpiece life, a life of purpose and peak performance that is able to withstand any outside force and still stand strong, is possible. But just like those structures, a life of peak performance won't happen by chance. The ONLY way it will happen is by intention, purpose-driven decisions, and consistent effort. It starts with a firm foundation. This chapter explains how to set the firm foundation needed to begin practicing purpose and peak performance, and it starts with the core formula.

CORE FORMULA: RESULTS = MY ACTIONS + GOD'S INPUT

Have you ever felt like despite all the work you are doing, you still aren't achieving the results you want? Have you ever felt like the weight of the world is on your shoulders? Like you are carrying so much (job, career, kids, marriage, etc.) that it literally feels like it's physically weighing you down? Have you ever felt frustrated and stressed out because you are trying to juggle so much on your own that you just wish you could catch a break before you literally breakdown? Have you ever felt like you are working so hard, but not really getting anywhere? Well, one of the first foundational principles that **must** be understood is that we are only in control of a certain portion of our lives, or better said, we do not control 100% of the outcomes and results in our lives—contrary to what you may think. This concept is very difficult for many of us driven professionals to understand and accept. It was difficult for me to come to grips with the fact that I am not in complete control of my life. In the fast-paced, results-based professional world (i.e. Corporate America), the "Get it done!" mentality is engrained in the culture, so when I bring up this idea, many people are like "What?" For anyone who loves to be in control (control freaks like myself) and feels more reassured and comfortable knowing "I'm in control," this can really be a struggle. I'd heard many clichés such as "If it is to be, it's up to me" and "I am the creator of my own destiny," and so forth and so on. And these phrases are not false, but they are not 100% true. You've got to add the words "…if that's what God wants" to each of these frequently used self-help mantras. I, for the longest, thought the equation was "My results = My actions," but this was a large part of the frustration, stress, average results, and lack of fulfillment in my life years ago. I tried carrying the weight of everything on my shoulders. I carried the weight of being successful in business, being the breadwinner, being a successful doctor, and the weight of so many other things that I was completely weighed down, unproductive, and unhappy. But, thanks to a mentor and friend, I was told to go to God and just let him have his part of my life, to surrender control and allow him to take care of his part of the equation. This, though difficult to do, eventually and drastically changed my perspective on everything I was trying so hard to control. More importantly, it drastically transformed my entire life! I concluded a few things from the core formula: (1) there is only one part of this formula that I can control—my actions and decisions. Nothing more, nothing less. (2) I cannot control God's input on the results and outcomes in my life. Therefore, I must simply focus on making sure I'm doing all I can do to maximize *my* actions and decisions and let God handle the rest. (3) I, no matter what, have personal responsibility for any and everything that happens in my life, because no matter what my actions are within the formula (even if I do nothing), it has an influence on the end result! As a result of coming to these conclusions, several amazing transformations happened. The first was that my stress level decreased, knowing the weight wasn't all on me! What a relief and huge weight off of my shoulders! What was interesting about coming to this conclusion was that my work ethic at the time didn't change, but I was getting better results. I began seeing improvement in my medical practice and direct sales business. I realized I was showing up different, less stressed and more optimistic, which had a hugely positive impact on my environment and productivity. It also made me much more aware and responsible for my actions and decisions because I knew those same actions and decisions would undoubtedly influence my results. This change also had a major positive effect on my spiritual life. I now relied more on God and his infinite ability rather than my own, knowing he is much more capable, of course.

When I think about how many of us want to control everything in our lives and try to put it all on our shoulders with no help, I think about being in the gym, working out alone. I want you to imagine lifting weights, bench pressing, and trying to do all the lifting on your own. You try to force your growth, putting so much weight on the bar that you can barely lift it, and become frustrated because you are not getting the results you want. Now imagine someone spotting you and helping you lift the weight, not so much that you don't do your part to get the weight up, but enough help so that you still grow and see results, without buckling from the pressure. I realized how much I was struggling on my own and when I put my pride aside and finally let God "spot me", I was immediately able to get the weight up much better, without the fear of it falling on me, but holding on to enough that I could still grow through the process. The result? More tangible success. Question: Where can you use a solid and reliable "spot" in your life? Where in your life are you trying to lift it all on your own and about to buckle under the pressure? Don't forget the core formula: Results = My actions + God's input. Remember, all we can control, as it comes to the results in our lives, is our actions and decisions. Since that is all we can control, then that is what we will primarily focus on for the rest of this book. God's got his part of the formula covered. We cannot control that. But let's set our attention to what we can control.

BREAKING DOWN DECISION-MAKING

Our actions, the portion of the equation that we can control and has the most direct effect on our results, are functions of our decisions. Any decision we make is directly associated with its expected action. To illustrate this, let's use a very simple example of dinner plans:

- Decision: It's dinner time and I decide to have pizza for dinner.
- Action: I go online to find the closest pizza restaurant and call to place a delivery order.
- Result: Pizza is delivered and then devoured for dinner.

Decision → Action → Result. Our decisions directly influence our results. Therefore, if you make different decisions, you get different results. This also means if you make **better decisions**, you get **better results**.

We are constantly making decisions—day-by-day, hour-by-hour, and minute-by-minute. Therefore, if we are constantly making decisions, and these decisions directly influence our results, then the goal we should have for our lives is to become the best decision-makers we can be to influence the results we ultimately desire. **Peak performance, both professionally and personally, requires being a great decision-maker for your life.**

How then, does the decision-making process work? Decisions are functions of two things, our "beliefs" and our "blueprint." Any decision we make, we take into account both what we believe (our "beliefs") and the knowledge we currently have (our "blueprint"). For example, I decide to call Pizza Company #1 to order the pizza because I believe they are the best value (belief) and because they are the closest pizza restaurant, that I'm aware of, that delivers in the area (blueprint). But let's say I was made aware of another pizza restaurant nearby, Pizza Company #2, which also delivers (new knowledge, i.e. blueprint) and it tastes better. Now, I believe the new pizza place has the best value around (belief), so when it's time to order pizza again, I'll decide to order from pizza company #2. Our minds deal with all decisions the same way, whether it concerns something as simple as deciding what to eat or as important as deciding to make a career change. For example, if you don't enjoy your current job and you really want to go after your passion of starting a food truck, but your belief is that you'll likely fail because someone you know failed at something similar, then you will likely decide not to start the food truck…even if you have a lot of knowledge about food and cooking. With that said, both the belief and blueprint influence the decisions we make. But, our belief influences the decisions we make to a much greater degree than our blueprint. We will discuss this more in depth shortly. But in order to practice peak performance professionally or personally, we must be the best possible decision makers for our lives and intentionally work on our beliefs and blueprints (i.e. reading, learning, and being open to experience and learn more and new things).

THREE PRINCIPLES FOR GREAT DECISION-MAKING

There are three key principles that elite-level performers understand and apply in order to make the decisions that lead to extraordinary results:

1) Seek help/coaching/mentoring/partnering.

This is essential and imperative in making the best decisions for your life. Other people have been where you are and have done what you are trying to do. They've already taken the road you are currently looking to take. Imagine going on a road trip and you know where you want to go to, but you've never traveled there before. You may have a map to assist you in getting there. However, you don't know where the gas stations are to refuel, where the speed traps are, the construction and detours. You don't know alternate routes of getting there if something unexpected happens on the road. However, imagine if you knew someone who happened to have taken that trip. They know where the potholes, construction, and speed traps are. They know where to refuel. They have reached the destination you seek. Therefore, you should seek their knowledge, wisdom, and expertise. Not to do so is foolish! Look at anyone with any significant results in their lives, albeit health, wealth, business, speaking, or otherwise. They received counsel, coaching, or mentorship from someone. Getting help does several things: (1) It increases productivity by minimizing mistakes and (2) increases efficiency by decreasing the time it takes to succeed. Two people working toward one task will always work faster and more efficiently than one person working on a task. (3) Accountability to take action. When in the company of others, you are more likely to take action toward your goals instead of procrastinating or making excuses. (4) Encouragement, motivation and support during the journey. During the times when the road gets bumpy and you want to quit, receiving encouragement and borrowing someone else's belief is always a great help. (5) Perspective to see the things that you can't. Too often we miss things because it is hard to see the full picture when you are in the frame. Someone else's ability to see the picture with you in it will provide clarity because they'll see things you cannot. You'll be able to avoid the same potholes they stepped in along the journey. Always seek help when you set a new goal or look to change or transform something in your life. As you start on your journey, the best way to find the appropriate help is to look for someone who has successfully accomplished what you are looking to achieve and then reach out to them.

2) Be teachable and coachable.

There are three areas of knowledge: 1) what we know, 2) what we don't know, and 3) what we don't know we don't know. For example, I know how to do specific procedures in my clinic to improve the health of my patients. Giving someone an injection in their joint would be an example. This would obviously fall into the category of "what I know." Second, there is "what I don't know." I know that I don't know how to pilot an airplane. Then there are things in this world that I don't even know that I don't know. By far, the smallest area of knowledge is what we do know. That said, there's a lot of knowledge we are completely unaware of, enough knowledge such that if we knew about it, could completely change the way we make decisions. Knowledge **is** power! Consider this. There was once a time when people smoked cigarettes and were clueless to the fact that it was a cause of cancer. Through research we gained the knowledge that it was literally killing people. This knowledge has been life changing, because without it, many more people would continue to engage in a habit that could lead to cancer. Also, something as simple as the act of handwashing in medicine was a massive discovery. Many people were dying from post-surgery infections prior to the discovery that bacteria was on our hands, and was playing a major role in the infections people suffered. The simple knowledge of the effectiveness of water and soap in killing bacteria ended up saving the lives of millions and has had a drastic effect on medicine ever since. I would consider this knowledge very powerful. Another way to think about it is that lack of knowledge is actually dangerous. Without the knowledge of cigarette's connection to cancer and the importance of washing bacteria off of your hands, many more people would die as a result! But the first step in acquiring new knowledge and expanding your blueprint is being **open** and **willing** to learn new information. Therefore, in order to make the best decisions for your life you must be willing and open to learn new information and just as willing to learn new things about the knowledge you currently have. This is the definition of being teachable, and being teachable goes a long way to being a great decision maker. Otherwise, you run the risk of lacking knowledge that could completely change the way you make a decision, and the results in your life.

For example, while in medical school I was on a radiology rotation, and the attending doctor who ran this rotation began explaining on day one that he was financially independent, saying the only reason he came to the hospital to teach us was because he enjoyed it, not because he needed the money. He then proceeded to tell us that if we wanted to learn the things he learned to become financially independent, we needed to read several books that he'd read, and he gave us the titles. I was 26 years old at the time and had zero financial education, not even sure how to make a budget. I was horrible with money. If I had it, I spent it. During that month rotation, I read the books he recommended. As a result, my life from then on was drastically changed with the knowledge I'd acquired from a three-minute discussion during a radiology rotation. I'd learned things I had no clue about—principles as simple as making a budget, living below my means, and saving money. Being teachable is essential for peak performance. Without it, you'll miss the lessons needed to learn to excel to a new level in your goals. I would still have poor spending habits and be unaware of how to accumulate wealth had I not been open and willing to learn something new. But once you are open and willing, you must consistently seek new knowledge. Once you learn something about a topic, reading it once is not good enough to reinforce the memory of it in your brain or your ability to put it into practice. You must then continue to learn. You must be consistent with learning. Learning is not a one-time activity, it is a lifetime pursuit, particularly if you want to achieve higher levels of success and fulfillment in your life. Reading personal finance books during medical school was a phenomenal start, but it ultimately led me to read more and learn more so that I could become a great money manager. Because of the continued learning, I was able to eliminate more than $150,000 of school debt in less than six years and accumulate wealth at the same time.

The other characteristic of being a great decision-maker is being coachable. I define coachability as the willingness to change or adjust a certain practice or way of life in order to achieve a certain goal. We've already discussed the idea of receiving help from someone who is qualified. However, being coachable means listening *and* putting into action their advice, coaching, and direction. It requires you to change some ways of thinking and even eliminate certain actions that aren't serving you well enough to achieve the results you desire. To make the best decisions toward your desired outcomes in life, you **must** be coachable. What are you willing to change or sacrifice in order for things to change? Being coachable means leaving pride and "my way" of doing things at the door. It means being a good student and apprentice. I remember taking a golf course in college. I'd learned some basic fundamentals of swinging the golf club from my college roommate prior to taking the course. Prior to enrolling in the golf class, my ability to hit the ball in the air was very inconsistent. The coach would tell me how to grip the club and would say, "Stop trying to kill the ball. Swing the club slower and easier." The problem was that when I tried to execute his lessons, it was so uncomfortable. I was so used to "my way" of doing it that I would never apply his coaching. How was I supposed to hit the ball far without trying to hit the heck out of it? So, I kept getting the same result, grounder after grounder. I'll never forget the first time I decided to listen to his instruction. I gripped the club like he'd said, deliberately softened my swing, and voila! Straight and far. The coach laughed. Once I was willing to be coachable and follow his instruction, despite how uncomfortable or counterintuitive it seemed, it worked. Without being coachable, you will continue getting the results you are getting. Without being coachable and willing to change, increasing your level of performance is virtually impossible! A simple change in my willingness to accept appropriate instruction resulted in immediate results. This does not just apply to golf lessons. To experience elevated levels of performance in anything, a high level of teachability and coachability is essential. In order to maximize your personal and professional performance, and live out the best version of yourself, it means being in a constant state of growth and learning, and that cannot happen with an unwillingness to change. One thing is for sure. Nothing will change if you change nothing, and one thing that must change is your perspective and way of doing things, or you run the risk of getting the same stunted results.

3) Understand that "belief" is more important than your "blueprint."

It's been shown that our beliefs have 90% influence on our results, compared to 10% influence from our blueprint (i.e. the "know-how"). Ninety percent! That means our beliefs play a significant role toward the decisions we make and ultimately, our results. Our beliefs drive who we are and what we do. We will discuss the influence belief has on our performance in the next chapter, but suffice it to say, our beliefs are much more important than our blueprint, and have much greater influence on our ability to be great decision makers.

If you gave someone detailed instructions, all the tools, manpower, and know-how to build a home from scratch, but the person doesn't believe they can build it, there is no chance that a home will ever be built. With a lack of belief, there's a lack of results. However, if you give someone no instructions and limited resources to build a home, but they have an absolute certainty in their ability to figure it out and get it done, then it's just a matter of time.

Big belief = Big results! Our belief is the GREATEST SOURCE OF POWER we control toward influencing our desired result. Mastering our beliefs is by far the most important factor in decision-making and therefore, our results! Never forget this statement: *You become what you believe!*

CORE FORMULA CHAPTER SUMMARY

1. Core Formula: Results = My Actions + God's Input
    1. Let God handle his part of your results.
    2. Focus primarily on your actions.
2. Decisions directly influence our results. Therefore, our goal is to become the best decision maker we can be for our life.
3. 3 Principles to great decision-making:
    1. Seek help in the form of coaching or mentoring.
    2. Be teachable and coachable.
    3. Understand that your beliefs are more important than your blueprint.

MANIFESTATION MINDSET

The mind is the key to everything that happens within the rest of the body. It is the mainframe by which the rest of the body will follow instructions. In order for lasting change to happen, this amazing source of power must be controlled and used with intention toward the results we desire. This chapter will explain how this amazing source of creative power works.

Have you ever wondered why someone is able to accomplish phenomenal achievements despite the odds against them? Ever wonder why someone with less talent and ability can out-perform someone with superior talent? For example, Stephen Curry is a guard in the NBA. He's certainly not the tallest, or the fastest, or the quickest. All odds, based on his physical ability, predicted that he might not even survive in the NBA. Coming out of high school, he only got a few scholarship offers and played for a smaller college. Despite this, he's set records in the NBA for 3-point shooting and has won the league's Most Valuable Player award. Have you ever wondered why, despite the fact that we all get the same 24 hours a day, some of us get far more done with that same 24 hours than others. The answer: Mindset. Whether positive or negative, strong or weak, good or bad, our mindset is the most influential force on our results. Nothing plays such a powerful role on who we currently are, the results we have, and who we become in the future, than our mindset. Our performance is directly related to our mindset. Performance is simply a results-based measurement of the strength of one's mindset and beliefs. This basically means, ***if you want to increase your performance, then increase your mindset.***

When you see someone performing at a high level achieving extraordinary results, it is a direct reflection of the strength of their mindset and belief. Our mind is like a muscle and belief is the strength of that muscle. In order for a muscle to grow and be healthy, it requires the right input of nutrition and exercise. Our mind is no different. Many of us don't do anything to keep our mind in shape. We are familiar with all the cliché lines like "mind over matter", but we don't apply this. The mind has the most powerful influence on our results and is the key to performing at a higher level, yet, most of us don't have a consistent practice to exercise our minds to become stronger so it can work better toward creating the results we desire. Many of us pay more attention to the maintenance of material things (i.e. washing our cars, cleaning our homes) than the exercise, maintenance, and advancement of the most important force that effects everything. Remember: you become what you believe! So, if you want to become something different, you must believe something different. Or better said, if you want better results, you must start exercising the mind and strengthening your beliefs! Many of us are just mentally out of shape. However, peak performance requires an understanding of how the mind works and consistently applying the practice of working our mental muscle, such that our beliefs then lead to the results we want.

MIND VS. SOIL

The mind is very similar to soil. Remember this simple equation: **input = output**. Whatever seed is planted in the soil (input) is what will eventually grow (output). The mind works the same way. Whatever beliefs you plant in the mind will manifest as a result later. Another way to put it is that whatever you sow (albeit seeds or beliefs), will grow. Here are some similarities between the mind and the soil: (1) both the mind and the soil's sole responsibility is to grow what is planted, and it does a really good job of growing *exactly* what is planted. Many of us don't like the results we are harvesting in our lives. But the reason those results are happening is because of the beliefs that were planted in the past. (2) The mind and soil have no control over what's planted. So who controls what's planted? We do! We are the farmers of our own mind. We decide what gets planted and what doesn't. However, all too often, many of us lack the intention of a prudent farmer. A good farmer who harvests lots of crops is one who protects, waters, and cultivates the soil. He intentionally plants the seeds of what he wants to grow from his soil, and therefore has an expectation of what will grow. If a farmer doesn't tend to the soil and does not have intention with what he sows, he'll never be able to consistently harvest a fertile crop, feed his family and/or make a living. The mind is the same way. It needs to be tended, protected, poured into, and cultivated. We should protect our minds from negativity that can have an adverse effect on our positive beliefs, much like a farmer protects his soil from weeds that can kill his harvest. We must pour into ourselves, i.e. "investing in ourselves", by reading books, seeking appropriate mentoring and coaching, and attending events that empower us and help us grow, much like the farmer pours water into the soil to help the seed grow. We must cultivate the mind and create an environment for it to have the best ability to thrive, much like the farmer tills the soil to give the seed the best possible environment for it to grow. We do this by being careful of the environments to which we expose our minds and intentionally place ourselves around people and in environments with positivity, support, and encouragement. If we don't do these things, we can expect the same result of a farmer that doesn't care for his soil, poor results! (3) Neither the mind nor the soil will grow anything other than what was sown. So, if you plant an apple seed, you can expect apple trees to grow. An apple seed will never produce peaches on the branches of its tree—only apples. In the same way, when you plant the belief in the mind that you cannot succeed, it will grow that exact result, in abundance! However, if you plant the undoubted certain belief of your ability to accomplish a certain goal, the fruition of that goal is inevitable. The only way to get a different result is to plant a different seed. Seeds of negativity, unbelief, and doubt will never yield a harvest of positivity, achievement and the results you desire. Want different results? Plant different seeds! (4) The more consistent and the greater the volume of seeds planted, the more fruit that will grow. If you plant twenty apple seeds, more apples will eventually grow, as opposed to planting one apple seed. Similarly, if you plant more negative beliefs than positive ones, it will undoubtedly produce more negative results than positive ones.

THE DECISION-MAKING SEQUENCE

Input → Beliefs → Thoughts → Feelings → Decisions → Actions → Results

This is the mind's decision-making sequence. Results are the fruit harvested from the belief of what was planted in the past. The reason most people don't create lasting change is because they try to change their results by simply changing their decisions. New Year's resolutions are a prime example. People want to lose weight, but only change their actions by deciding to eat better and go to the gym more often. Trying to change your results by simply changing at the level of the decision does not go deep enough into the root of the mind to change an already deeply rooted belief of poor eating and minimal exercise that made them overweight in the first place. You must go further back in the sequence of the mind's decision-making in order to create lasting change, as far back as the belief that was planted. If you try to change your results only by changing at the level of your decisions, it is the equivalent of walking up to an apple tree, picking off an apple, then super-gluing a peach on the branch, and saying you want peaches to start growing from that branch. Sounds silly, right? Well that's what many of us try to do whenever we want to change a behavior or get a different result. We only go back as far as our decisions, but you must go back to where the seed was planted. If you try to change a behavior after the seed of a certain belief is planted and is already sprouting, it will continue to sprout the same result of the original belief planted. *At the root of any undesired result (for example, being overweight) is a "belief" problem, not an "action" problem.* In their mind exists both the lack of belief that they can be healthier, and an overwhelming belief and perception that they are an overweight individual. The belief about themselves, their ability, diet, and exercise must change in order for the end result to change. In the New Year's resolution example, most people don't go back far enough in the sequence to be able to make lasting change. This is why by the end of January, the gym is less crowded again. All of the people who only tried to change their actions to lose weight, have already quit, and the change in their behavior was temporary. This serves true for anything in life for which you want to create lasting, sustainable change and results. The beliefs planted in the mind (the input) must change in order to change a result. For example, my belief, for the vast majority of my life, was that I was not a morning person. I could not stand mornings! This belief resulted in very sluggish, unmotivated, and unproductive mornings for me. I constantly snoozed my alarm and would wake up so tired that it felt like it took the majority of the morning for me to wake up. For my entire life, if the topic of getting up early ever came up, I would always say, "I'm NOT a morning person! I don't do mornings." I even remember saying, "Me and mornings are like oil and water." I labeled myself a "night owl." However, there came a time when I wanted to be more productive with my day and perform at a higher level. I began noticing that highly productive people, high achievers, were early risers. They were "morning people." I'd read a book recommended to me by a friend, about how much more productive you can be by becoming a "morning person." Also, a mentor and friend who is very successful, productive, and a high achiever, often mentioned how he always gets up early in the morning. After reading the book and hearing my mentor's thoughts on getting up early, I decided to change my bad morning habits and turn into a "morning person." The problem was, I was a "night owl." But I knew that in order for my poor morning habits and sluggishness to change, I couldn't just start setting my alarm earlier in the morning in an attempt to try to get up early. I was going to have to couple that action with inputting a different belief into my mind. I wanted to be more productive, full of energy, and get more stuff done in the morning. I began intentionally planting new input into my mind (reading a book on morning routine; saying daily affirmations on how I enjoy the mornings and I am a morning go-getter), and over the course of two months, I consistently got up earlier, which for me was 5:30 a.m. every morning. As a matter of fact, getting up earlier has become such a habit now, I can't help but get up early! It just doesn't feel right to sleep in. Now, when I have the conversations I used to have about rising early, I describe myself as a "morning person." A change of belief, resulted in a change in results, and this can be done with intention to create lasting positive change in your life. To practice peak performance, it requires the understanding that it takes more than a change in your actions to create *lasting, sustainable* results. In order to change the fruit, you've got to change the root!

The interesting thing is, we verbalize our beliefs all the time. Here are a few you may have heard:

- "My day cannot get started until I have my morning cup of coffee!"
- "I have a bad memory."
- "I could never get in that kind of shape."
- "I'm not smart enough to do that."
- "I can't stop smoking."
- "I just simply can't seem to figure it out!"

The list goes on. These comments are actually deep seeded beliefs that are in the mind, come out of our mouths, and result in poor performance. Listening to these statements, there is no wonder why the person saying them gets exactly what they say (a dependency on coffee for a productive morning; a poor memory; a body that is out of shape; a mind that is not smart enough; the inability to stop smoking; an inability to figure out solutions to their problems). Peak performance requires a keen awareness of what you say. Words possess great power!

They have the power to build up as well as break down and therefore, we must use our words carefully because we believe what we say. Elite-level performance requires the understanding that what you express verbally is simply a reflection of what you believe internally. One of the earliest ways of knowing that one's beliefs are changing is that they begin talking different. What are some beliefs you verbally express that you aren't proud of and aren't serving you well? It could be in regard to your health, finances, relationships, spirituality or any aspect of your life. Write them down. The next couple of chapters will show you how to change these beliefs to ones that will optimally serve you, and promote positive, lasting change.

IMPORTANCE OF INPUT

When you look at the decision-making sequence, the way to harvest new results is to plant new seeds of belief in the mind. Input is the process of planting new beliefs that will then foster the subsequent thoughts → actions → decisions → and ultimately results. Therefore, we've got to get good at inputting appropriate beliefs that correlate with our desired result. Peak performance requires an understanding of the decision-making sequence and how to apply the input of appropriate beliefs to achieve results.

There are a few things to remember when inputting beliefs in your mind. First, begin with the end in mind. Have a firm idea of what result you want to harvest and then input the belief of your achievement of it in your mind, as if you've already achieved it. For example, I wanted to be a morning person that was more productive, looked forward to the morning, woke up with energy, and had a consistent morning routine that included exercise. Therefore, I began to input and program thoughts such as:

- "I enjoy the morning!"
- "I am full of energy and ready to take on the day when I wake up!"
- "I enjoy when my alarm goes off because I'm blessed with a new day."

Second, the input that you intentionally program/plant into your mind will create a belief that will lead to thoughts and feelings that are congruent with decisions, leading to your desired result. For example, as I started to input new beliefs of being a morning person in my mind, I began to have more thoughts of increased productivity, starting my day earlier, and all the benefits of being a morning person. Those thoughts led to an overall excitement and positive feeling about mornings now. Those positive feelings then more easily and consistently led to the decision to wake up and start my day earlier. That same decision then led to the desired result—being a person that consistently gets up early in the morning and is more productive, i.e. "a morning person"! So remember The Decision-Making Sequence: Input → Belief → Thoughts → Actions → Decision → Action → Result. But when it comes to what to input, begin with the end result you desire in mind.

You must also remember that in order to create lasting change toward your desired outcome, your feelings must match your actions. For example, if you want to lose weight, you will need to execute the "actions" of new lifestyle changes, including more exercise and healthier eating. Now, let's say you make these changes. If you still have negative feelings about exercise, with thoughts like "I hate working out," "I hate going to the gym," and "I don't like eating healthy," then those negative feelings toward the actions, are not congruent with weight loss. *Remember this, the mind won't consistently take action toward something it does not enjoy or has a negative feeling toward.* You can't want to lose weight, but hate working out. You can't want to become wealthy, but hate to have a budget. You can't want to have a happier marriage, but hate date night. In order for an action *to consistently* be carried out, you must have a positive feeling about that action. So remember, if you want **lasting** change, your feelings must match your actions toward your transformation. The more you enjoy exercise and healthy eating habits, the more successful you'll become in your weight loss goals. The only way to do that is to input new beliefs in your mind.

Third, there are two large categories of input for our minds: external and internal. External includes the audio and visual input that comes from the environments we are exposed to, both intentionally and subconsciously. This includes the music we listen to, the television we watch, conversations we hear, and the things we see and read. Internal input includes our self-talk and the internal discussions that play in our own minds. Both external and internal input influence the beliefs in our mind. However, ***the absolute most powerful form of***

input is internal, in the form of self-talk. The mind loves to hear its own voice, therefore the most powerful form of self-talk is verbal self-talk—actually hearing ourselves communicate with ourselves. So be careful what you hear yourself say, because the mind will begin to believe it. We are surrounded by different input all the time. However, the more consistent and direct the input, the more likely that belief will be planted securely in our minds to grow to fruition later. Here are the peak performance steps to input beliefs into your mind:

Creating Self-Talk Affirmations

1. Visualize in full detail and great imagination the best possible version of your desired result and outcome. Remember to begin with the end in mind.
    - What does your end goal look like? Employ all senses (smell, taste, hear, feel, and see).
    - What do you look like in this vision of your goal?
    - What are you doing different then from what you do now?
    - What characteristics and traits do you have that are different now?
    - How would you describe yourself to someone else?
    - What impact are you having?
    - How do you feel?
    - What actions are being taken in the vision of the accomplishment of your goal?

2. Write it down – Describe your vision in full detail. Answer the questions above and write them down as it relates to the vision of your accomplished goal! Remember, be vivid in your description!

   a. Write out each affirmation

      o Take what was written in step 2 and make them into affirmations

      o Use definitive and current vocabulary (e.g. I *am*, I *speak*, I *enjoy*, I *do*, etc., not, I will or I try). For example: "I AM a morning person"; "I AM a go-getter!"; "I ENJOY waking up early, ready to go after my day!"

      o Affirmations should be positive. Avoid negative affirmations toward your goal. For example, a negative affirmation would be, "I hate eating chocolate" and an alternative positive affirmation would be, "I enjoy making healthy decisions in my diet, and enjoy chocolate in very small, limited amounts"

      o Affirmations should build your belief in several areas. They are intended to build a positive belief in:

         ▫ Your ability/capability to accomplish your goal (i.e. I am strong; I am able; I am willing; I am confident; I can, etc.)

- ☐ The Process of attaining your goal (i.e. I enjoy reading; I am excited about…; I am hard-working etc.)
- ☐ Transformation – You must believe in the possibility of change (I am a healthy individual; I am debt-free; etc.)
- ☐ The reality of your vision – you must believe that your vision *is* reality, and it's only a matter of time (i.e. I am a great public speaker; I am a published author; etc.)

3. Voice Record the affirmations (repeat each one 3-5 times).
   - Read and record your affirmations with emotion, as if you are currently living the result you desire
   - These affirmations are the input, the seed, with which you will plant solid roots of belief into your mind

4. Identify the different external inputs around you, ones you can control whether or not to give your attention. Remember, these inputs influence your beliefs. Identifying them will allow you to see the inputs you need to replace and intentionally plant new, more productive ones. Example: music, television, conversations at work, things you read, environments like church, seminars, etc.
   - Write down the different inputs that you are aware of

5. Schedule times during the day when you will recite or listen to the recorded affirmations. Remember, the more you plant these seeds of belief that you desire, the more

likely you will achieve the desired result! Listen to each affirmation with the intent to believe it!

PEARLS AND PITFALLS

Pearls

1. Cultivate the soil/mind:
   a. Surround yourself with positive and uplifting people
   b. Read and invest in yourself for personal growth and development
      o Books, audios, seminars
   c. Listen to uplifting positive music
2. Become emotionally connected to your affirmations. This is your life! Your future! The input to the eventual attainment of your goals! You should get excited about that!
3. Envision the future outcome you desire and create a certain belief as though you are experiencing its fruition NOW!
4. Never forget your belief is much more influential than your blueprint (what you know)
5. Consistency despite the lack of visible results
   a. You must consistently continue to practice these principles, even when the results aren't yet there.
   b. Remember, these principles are setting the firm

foundation on which your hopes and dreams will be built. They are the roots to the tree. Often, you won't see any sprouting on the surface when a tree is planted because it must first grow strong and deep roots that will become sturdy enough to hold up a massive tree that will bear much fruit. So trust that growth is happening even though you don't see it. It's called the "invisible growth." It's the growth of the roots and foundation before tangible results happen. Stay consistent! It's happening, even if you can't see it yet!

c. Be patient. Expect this new process to be awkward and uncomfortable in the beginning. Just like anything new you are learning, there is a learning curve. Think about going through this process of belief input as starting a new workout in the gym. Day 1, week 1, and even month 1 is a little awkward and uncomfortable. It takes some time to get your routine and muscle memory down until you are in a groove. It also takes several weeks before any real results are seen. It's the same for successfully inputting new beliefs in your mind. Your mind, as mentioned before, is like a muscle. The more you exercise this muscle consistently, the stronger the belief becomes. The initial practice of belief input will be awkward and uncomfortable at first, and you may not see results initially, but once you get your routine and mindset down, it's only a matter of time then! And just like a muscle, if the mind gets neglected and isn't consistently exercised with repetitions of intentional belief input, it will gradually become weak and perform poorly. Therefore, to practice a high level of performance, you must do repetitions daily toward directed belief input in your mind, as outlined above.

Pitfalls

1. Not giving attention to and caring for "the soil", i.e. your mind

2. Inconsistency in input, which will eventually lead to inconsistent results.

3. Not generating an emotional connection to the belief

4. Not mentally experiencing your future vision in the present

5. Getting distracted by current circumstances:
   - Don't get distracted by your current circumstances. They **will** change toward your result as long as you remain consistent.

6. Getting inpatient with no results

7. Remember, the roots and foundation take the longest time to grow, but must be grown first!
   - Worrying about "The How", i.e. the blueprint, and the NOW.

MINDSET MANIFESTATION CHAPTER SUMMARY

- Performance is simply a results-based measurement of the strength of one's mindset and belief.
- If you want to increase your performance, improve your mindset!
- The mind is similar to soil:
  - Input = Output
  - The beliefs you plant now will later harvest equal results.
- The decision-making sequence:
  - Input→Beliefs→Thoughts→Feelings→Decisions→Actions→Results
  - At the root of any undesired result is a "belief" problem, not an "action" problem
  - The thoughts you express verbally is simply a reflection of what you believe internally. Be aware and careful of what you say!
- Input
  - The mind won't consistently take action toward something it does not enjoy or has a negative feeling toward. Therefore, you should have positive feelings about the actions required to create results.
  - The most powerful form of input is self-talk!

- When creating self-talk affirmations:
  - Visualize your future result. Begin with the end in mind.
  - Write it down in great detail.
  - Create self-talk affirmations from what was written in step 2.
  - Voice record the affirmations.
  - Schedule times to listen to them throughout the day.

CLEAR PURPOSE

One of the main practices of peak performance is the pursuit of a clearly defined purpose. It also means you must be living out, or pursuing your life's purpose. Therefore, if you are not currently pursuing what you believe to be your purpose, you must now define what that is. Clarity on your purpose will help with multiple areas of your life, including goal achievement, priority management, and happiness. With clarity of your purpose comes the confidence to then pursue it, which results in a greater feeling of significance, contribution, and service. Ultimately, in order to experience genuine overall fulfillment, the discovery and pursuit of your purpose is vital.

DISCOVERING YOUR PURPOSE

God has a specific purpose that you are meant to fulfill on this earth. It is your calling. It's the role you are meant to play, the piece of the puzzle you are meant to fill in order for the full picture to make sense and the world to go round. The question is, do you know what your purpose is? What your role is? What piece of the puzzle you are contributing to the larger picture? Can you answer these questions clearly? Most people are unable to answer these questions with confidence. If we don't know our purpose, we suffer from a lack of clarity in our lives. This leads to frustration, and feeling lost and unproductive. Imagine playing basketball, and you don't know what position you are playing or what your role and responsibilities are when you are on the court. You don't know the plays, who to pass the ball to, or how and who to defend. Every time you get the ball it's either a turnover or missed shot because you are unaware of what you are supposed to be doing. You can imagine that you'd be frustrated, feel lost, and wouldn't be maximizing your full talent since you don't know your purpose for being on the court. You couldn't contribute like you would if you knew your role and purpose on the team. Not only does this affect you, but it affects those around you. Your team doesn't get the best chance of winning. When you don't live in your purpose, not only does it mean feeling lost and frustrated, but it often results in someone else not being able to experience a better life because your purpose is unfulfilled. You see, many of us have this voice in the back our heads, that intuition that "there's something else out there for me!" That voice is the call that you need to answer in order to go after and fulfill your purpose. For example, when you finally address that voice, spend intentional time finding your purpose and take action to fulfill it, there's a certain level of fulfillment that comes simply from the discovery and pursuit of your purpose. We all want to feel significant and part of that comes from our level of contribution. When you live in and go after your purpose, you contribute your piece to the larger puzzle. You contribute to the team and therefore find significance and fulfillment in that. You feel like you matter! However, many of us choose to ignore that voice for whatever reason. Either we believe it's not going to make us enough money, that it's going to take too much time, or that it will require us to sacrifice our time, current career, or even some deep-seeded beliefs we comfortably hold on to. No matter the reason, when you ignore this purpose-driven "voice" that's calling, it always, ALWAYS costs you more if you ignore it than if you address it. You **must** answer the call. Otherwise, you run the risk of regret, knowing there's a purpose you were supposed to fulfill and because you decided to ignore it, someone does not get to be blessed by your courage to go after it.

My definition for pursuing your purpose is *the application of your gifts and talents, fueled by your passions and past experiences, to serve others by providing value to improve their lives.* Your purpose must include service to others. It's not your purpose if it doesn't help others to improve their lives. Thank God there have been people who have had the courage to answer "the call" and pursue their purpose. The local baker, the restaurant owner, the motivational speaker, the pastor, the technology company owner—because of them we get to experience better lives in the form of delicious food, awesome inspiration, spiritual education, and cellular phones. So the question is, what is your purpose? What is your contribution to the service and improvement of other's lives? Let's find it and go after it, because if not, there's a large group of people who won't get to experience the blessing you were meant to serve them.

Here are some steps on finding your purpose:

Gifts/Talents

Identify and write down your gifts and talents. What are things that come natural for you? What is something that is easy for you to do? What have people mentioned how good you are at doing? What is something that you think you are really good at doing? What's a skill, trait, or characteristic that people compliment you about?

Passions

Identify and write down your passions. What do you love doing? What would you do or what do you already do to help someone for free? What do you really enjoy? What are your hobbies? What activities make you joyful or happy? What could you see yourself doing or talking about EVERYDAY for the next 5 years?

Accomplishments

Make a list of all the things you have accomplished (trophies, certificates, courses, higher education, awards, etc.).

Challenges

What are some challenges you have overcome? What was a problem you had that you were able to find a solution for and successfully solve? What's been a memorable trial or test in your life that you now have a testimony for? What difficult or dark time in your life did you go through and overcome, and because of it you learned something and you are now a better person because of it? What are some life lessons you have learned that you could reliably teach others?

Things you don't want others to experience

What have you experienced in your life that you would hate to have someone else experience if you could help it? What have you been through, such that you could help successfully guide someone else to get through the same struggle? What have you learned and applied to your life that has been an absolute life-changer and that you would want to educate someone else on so it would have a similar impact on their life? What has impacted your life in such a positive way, that sharing that same message or experience with someone else would bring you joy if they had the same result.

Tying it all together

Remember the definition of pursuing your purpose: ***It's the application of your gifts and talents, fueled by your passions and past experiences, to serve others by providing value to improve their lives.*** Look at the answers to all the questions above and identify the common threads. Which ones really speak to you and are drawing you to it? Which answer really draws forth an emotional connection? Once you've done this, you are on your way to identifying your **Fundamental Purpose Statement**. A Fundamental Purpose Statement is a clear description and way to communicate your purpose. It describes three things: (1) Who you are serving or helping, (2)

How you are helping them, and (3) What the person's transformation is as a result of you helping those people. Be able to fill in the blanks of this sentence:

- I help _____ (define the group of people),
- by _____ (define how you are going to help them),
- so they can _____ (define the transformation they'll experience as a result of your service).

For example, my Fundamental Purpose Statement is: I help busy professionals by maximizing their performance, so they can experience professional success and personal fulfillment at the same time. Practice this statement, write several versions of it until it fits. Discuss it with other people and get their input. Write it down, erase it, and tweak it over and over until it fits what you feel is the best description of your purpose. Don't get discouraged if it doesn't come right away. It's okay! Discovering a clear purpose takes some time, trial and error, and patience. However, it's worth it and is one of the key steps toward your fulfillment and increased performance.

YOUR WHY

Once you've discovered a clear purpose, you must then identify why you are going after it. To perform at a high level you **must** have a strong, deep-seeded "why." The "why" is important because if it is strong enough, it will be the reason you continue pushing toward your purpose when times get tough. The why should be something that is bigger than you, bigger than any superficial or material things, and be rooted in service and positive impact for others. The strongest "why" is often connected to people—not letting them down, serving them, and impacting their lives in ways that your own life was impacted. Your "why" will be connected to the people you are serving as part of your purpose. For example, if your why to get in better shape is because you want to look good in a swimsuit for the beach, there is nothing wrong with that. But what happens after you've hit your goal for the beach? Often, the motivation to sustain that change is gone. A much better and lasting "why" would be to remain healthy, serve as a great example of health for your family, and be able to live a healthy life long enough to experience as much time with your family on this earth as possible! That is a strong why, because if you don't make better choices for your health, then someone else is let down. Here's a great question to ask yourself as you are formulating your why: *Who or what individuals will suffer as a result of you not doing what you are personally responsible for in the pursuit of your purpose?* Write this answer down. When you figure this out, use the answer to this question to be the motivating force behind what you are going after. It will help you get past those times when you are unmotivated to take action—and that happens to the best of us.

My answer to that question is: If I don't pursue my purpose of instructing and inspiring others how to live a successful and fulfilling life, there will be individuals out there who will continue to suffer from stress, a lack of belief, poor results, a lack of purpose and fulfillment, and will never get to experience the best version of themselves because I decided to not write my book, or record my video, learn how to be a better speaker, etc. This answer is my "why"! It's what motivates me when I get discouraged, when the journey gets difficult, or when I'm challenged with a problem. I propels me to keep moving because not only can I not let myself down, but I surely can't let down those people who are waiting for my blessing, and you should feel the same way about your "why" and the people waiting for your service to improve their lives!

SELF-EVALUATION – AM I DOING THE RIGHT THING? AM I OUT OF POSITION?

When it comes to our career and even certain goals we are pursuing, many of us are playing out of position. What I mean by that is, we all have gifts, talents, and passions, but we are in a career or going after a goal that doesn't draw upon the best of our gifts, talents, and passions. When you are going after something that employs what comes naturally, you don't have the feeling of dreading your work. You are excited to work. Your work is easier because not only do you have a stronger desire to do it, you have more fun doing it and the work is literally easier for you.

Imagine this. Many of us are like Shaquille O'Neal, a 7ft 300lb center with tons of talent as a center on the basketball court, trying to play point guard, completely out of position and not taking full advantage of our innate gifts and talents. This often happens because we see someone else being successful or we are drawn to go after something because we see others creating results, and maybe earning more money, by living a certain lifestyle. But we never stop to think that the reason that person is having success is because they are playing in their position, a position that maximizes their gifts, talents, passions! However, that doesn't mean it's the same position you should be playing. You have your own set of unique gifts and talents that can be maximized in a different position.

However, I've seen people playing out of position all too often. How often have you heard that someone went into real estate because they saw a friend doing well in real estate? Or someone started a home-based business because they saw their friend doing well in the same home-based business? Instead of making the decision to become a realtor or direct sales business owner based on a firm knowledge of their gifts and talents, they make the decision based on the results they see someone else having and that they want. On the surface this seems very logical. But this often times is a set up for "playing out of position" in their career or business, characterized by frustration, poor performance, and unfulfillment. Instead of choosing, or even continuing, a certain career or business based on identifying and attempting to duplicate a certain result (such as earning a certain income or lifestyle), you should rather clearly identify your gifts and talents and then find a way to practice and apply those gifts to create the results you desire.

In the above scenario, someone looking to make extra income should instead identify what their gifts, talents, passions, and past experiences are to come up with ideas of making extra income by applying those things, and if it happens to be real estate or direct sales, then great! I have nothing at all against real estate or home-based businesses. I actually believe both are phenomenal businesses. I'm simply using them as examples to make the point that the career you pursue should be based on your natural abilities, not on someone else's purpose-driven results. Otherwise, you are much more likely to find yourself in a career or business where you are "playing out of position." The reality is people are playing out of position in almost every career and business that exists.

A self-evaluation and personal inventory of your experiences and abilities allows you to really consider whether or not you are positioned in the best way possible to use your gifts and passions to be successful, maximize your results, and experience fulfillment in your life. The simplest way to maximize your performance is to play to your strengths! Use the gifts you've been blessed with! Simply deciding a career or goal based on the success of others or what "sounds good" is not enough. Going after a career and goals that position us best to utilize our gifts not only gives us the likelihood to be successful, but also to experience more fulfillment. Find what you are good at, how you can serve others with it, and a strong reason why you are doing it, then go after it!

FRAMEWORK TO SAY "NO"

Identifying your gifts, talents, passions, and ultimately your purpose, gives you a framework with which to make decisions. Opportunities come our way all the time. Opportunities are everywhere. But knowing your purpose and your "why" helps filter those opportunities you should look closer into, and ones you should say "No, thank you" to. If it's in line with your purpose and your "why", then it's likely something that will fit you and best position you to be successful. Ultimately, when it comes to your career and business, there should only be one or two things that you decide to put your heart and soul into, until you eventually have more time freedom to pursue other interests. Many people spread themselves too thin, trying to put lots of effort in multiple things. By knowing your purpose, you gain clarity on that which you should put your heart into and things that are more side projects that don't require as much of your effort. In order to perform at an elite level, you cannot be spread too thin. It requires narrowing your pursuit to a couple of ideas that earn your attention. Once you've narrowed down those ideas you can then master your craft, sharpen your skills, and further develop your gifts and talents to create more value. Only once you've mastered those ideas, should you expand your interests. But this begins by having a great framework to say "no" and make decisions hinged upon your identified gifts, talents, passions, and past experiences.

CLEAR PURPOSE CHAPTER SUMMARY

- God has a specific purpose you are meant to fulfill on this earth
- Pursuing your purpose is the application of your gifts, fueled by your passions and past experiences, to serve others by providing value to improve their lives.
- Fundamental Purpose Statement:
  - It's a clear description and way to communicate your purpose. It describes three things:
    - Who you are serving/helping?
    - How you are serving/helping them?
    - What is the person's transformation as a result of you serving/helping them?
- Your "why"
  - Should be connected to something bigger than you
  - A strong "Why" should be connected to service of others
  - "Who will suffer as a result of you not doing what you are personally responsible for in the pursuit of your purpose?" The answer to this question should be a part of your "why."
- Self-evaluation
  - Avoid "playing out of position" in your career or

business by identifying your gifts, talents, passions and past experiences and pursuing a path that will allow you to apply and grow these traits.

- Framework to say "No"
    - Only focus your attention on a few things that really take advantage of your gifts, passions, talents, and past experiences. If an opportunity doesn't provide the application and growth of these things, then consider politely declining.

DEFINED GOALS

Many people dream of what their life could be like, but not many people intentionally ask, "How can I create the life I dream of?" When designing the life you desire, you should always start with the end in mind. Another way to frame this is, when designing the life you desire, you should begin with a specific destination. You should have a clear vision of what the end goal should look, feel, and be like. For example, before you get in the car to go anywhere, you typically know where it is you are going. You know the end destination before you begin the journey. You can also use the GPS to identify the location of the specific address you are seeking. Without a clear vision of how you want your professional and personal life to look, there is little chance you'll experience a life of success or fulfillment. Whether personally or professionally, peak performance requires that you have a clear vision of what you want and defined step-by-step goals on how to achieve it. A unique way to look at this is to compare your vision and goals to a journey toward a destination. Imagine your vision of your future life as the destination, and the goals you define to get there are the different rest stops along the way. A lack of vision and defined goals would be like getting in a car and starting to drive, but with no true destination. That experience would be filled with frustration, purposeless turns and aimless driving, leaving the driver completely lost with no direction. This is unfortunately how many people are living, with no true understanding of what they want or where they are going. This chapter will give you an understanding of how elite-level performers start with the vision of their destination and create a roadmap of goals for how to get there.

7 PILLARS OF PEAK PERFORMANCE

There are seven major pillars, or categories, of our lives that we have a personal responsibility towards advancing and maintaining. The decisions we make within each of these pillars collectively contribute to who we are as a whole. No matter what decisions we make on a daily basis, it influences one of these pillars someway or somehow. Peak performance requires not only an awareness and understanding of each of these pillars, but also requires that a clear vision be defined for each pillar. These seven pillars include:

1. Spirituality
2. Marriage/Family/Relationships
3. Purpose/Calling
4. Career
5. Health
6. Wealth
7. Personal Interests (i.e. hobbies, things you enjoy doing)

Each of these categories translates to one of the many hats we happen to wear at any given time in our lives. In order to perform at a high level, experience more fulfillment, and live the absolute best version of ourselves, we must be both aware of and appropriately prioritize our time within each of these pillars. However, because of our lack of awareness and poor priority management, we find ourselves neglecting significant areas of our lives. This results in increased stress and frustration, and decreased productivity and feelings of being overwhelmed. For example, many of us have a robust career and wealth but suffer spiritually, in our relationships and our health. This example is unfortunately, an all too common combination in our current professional community. It's what I define as a "successful unfulfilled professional", the professional who has successfully reached all the outward signs of success, at the cost of their fulfillment. Many of us professionals thought that fulfillment would be paired with the accomplishment of our professional career, then felt bamboozled when it wasn't. The result is feeling stuck and trapped. I believe it's time to place a premium on the pursuit of fulfillment **first,** then trust and believe that we can still experience success professionally. Otherwise, what's the point of being successful professionally if it's not personally fulfilling?

Another example of "pillar mismanagement" includes someone who may be successful in their career and in great health, but still secretly struggles with living check to check, and feeling like they aren't living in their purpose. Whatever it is, many of us have between 1 and 4 areas that could use some real help. But the question is, can you actually get it all done? Can you live a life of overall high performance, a life of success both personally and professionally? Is a life of success **and** fulfillment even possible?" The answer is YES! It means maximizing your performance, professionally and personally. It requires that a vision, goals, priority management, and a plan of action be applied to **each** pillar in order to experience more productivity, less stress, and live out the best version of yourself.

DEFINING DAILY GOALS TO ACHIEVE YOUR VISION

Each pillar of your life should have a "vision statement." This statement should include a vivid description of how you envision that area of your life to be. Select any pillar and start thinking in depth about the vision you have for this area of your life. For each pillar, ask:

- "How do I want my spiritual relationship with God to look?"
- "How do I want my marriage to be?"
- "How do I want the fulfillment of my purpose to look like?"
- "How do I want my career to look like?"
- "How do I envision the healthiest version of me?"
- "How do I want my wealth and finances to look?
- "What hobbies and personal interests would I like to maintain?

Start with the pillar that presents the most challenges for you. Write your vision statement and remember the word "intention." Without intentionally declaring how you want a pillar of your life to look, you lack vision. With no vision there is no direction. And with no direction, there is no chance of that pillar of your life having successful and desired results. For each pillar, go through steps 1-5 in the Chapter 2, under "Importance of Input" and describe in full detail what you and your life look like in each pillar.

Now that the vision is clear, it's time to BELIEVE IT! Remember, *you become what you believe.* Therefore, in order for each pillar's vision to come to fruition, we must begin to apply what we've learned about the input of new beliefs into our mind. Begin to input, via self-talk and intentional cultivation of the mind, the seeds of belief needed to harvest the future you desire. Once the vision of the pillar is clear and you are working toward its belief, it's now time to reverse engineer the result.

REVERSE ENGINEERING

Now that the vision of how you want each pillar to look is clear and described in detail, we must answer the question, "What steps do I need to take to get there?" Each of the "steps" that we outline is a long, middle, and short-term goal that you will need to clearly define. Your short, middle, and long-term goals are like the landmarks and rest stops that must be visited along the way to the destination. For example, I can remember as a child that during the holidays our family would drive from Houston to Lake Charles, Louisiana to visit my grandparents. Along the way I remember passing a specific billboard in Orange, TX, and we would stop at McDonald's in Beaumont, TX. There was a bridge we would drive across going from TX to Louisiana, and a gas station we would pass once in Lake Charles before we eventually we got to my grandparents' house. I compare the short, middle, and long-term goals to the landmarks and stops I defined on the journey we took during the holidays. The end vision that I clearly define is compared to the end destination of my grandparents' home. Set the destination first, and then define the steps, i.e. goals necessary to get there. This is your roadmap. Examples:

- Roadmap Outline for Wealth Pillar:
    - Vision: To be debt free
        - Long-Term Goal – All debts paid off
        - Mid-Term Goal – Student loans paid off
        - Short-Term Goal – Create a budget; Pay off highest interest credit card first
- Roadmap Outline for Career Pillar:
    - Vision: Large Promotion
        - Long-Term Goal – Senior management position
        - Mid-Term Goal – Top 5 in Sales in company
        - Short-Term Goal – Increase the amount of monthly sales calls

Now understand, this is a roadmap we are creating, a game plan. The path to your final destination, i.e. your vision, often changes because of construction, detours, or unexpected weather, so sometimes it requires a different route than what is written and defined on the roadmap. Therefore, sometimes it takes us longer to get to there. We may even need to adjust the directions on the roadmap or reroute the path on the GPS. But let it be clear that ***regular adjustments and changes made to the roadmap to get to our destination are to be expected!*** It's part of the natural process of the journey. Do not make the mistake of perceiving an adjustment as confirmation that the destination is no longer achievable. Sometimes even the destination must be adjusted, but is still very much achievable. Many people will interpret a change in direction or a detour on the roadmap as a reason to quit or a sign that they can no longer reach their final destination. Please understand, the journey **must** be mapped out, not because it will always be followed road for road, but so that you will have a framework with which to begin, take action, and eventually adjust or "course correct." When I make a roadmap to reach my visions, my goals are like landmarks that I intend to reach along the way, but I expect the unexpected red light, road construction, or detour in my process of getting there. It's called unexpected circumstances, or life! It happens. But it certainly doesn't mean the destination is no longer possible to reach. A detour is just that—a detour, not a "STOP" sign. If anything, see it as a blessing that plans had to change in order to get you to your goal, because it may have otherwise been a dead end. This is why you should never worry about "how" you will reach your goal. "How" you reach your goal will almost never happen the way you think. The real path almost never follows the exact roadmap, but you'll need defined goals and a plan in order to begin. To practice peak performance, you **must** learn to take your visions, define goals to get there, take action, and adjust your roadmap along the way.

After you've identified each goal needed to reach your end destination, you must then quantify each goal based on time, volume, or quantity. For example: If I'm looking to lose weight and be healthier, I must quantify by deciding how much weight I would like to lose, and by what time. This is like putting a specific address in the GPS. Think about it. A GPS works best when you provide a specific address. Your goals are best reached when you quantify them with specific information. If you quantify your goals by deciding that you want to lose 50lbs in two months, be debt free in two years, or make 20 sales in three months, you now have something specific to aim toward. However, this becomes kind of scary for some people because of the accountability that immediately comes with these kinds of goals. It may also spark the fear of failing to reach your goal. However, what I urge you to understand is that goals are quantified, not because something bad will happen if you don't reach them, but so you will know how to course-correct. Remember, your path on the roadmap will need adjustments, but you won't know what adjustments to make without defined goals, followed by the action toward reaching them. You may find that for your schedule, losing 50lbs in two months is too much. This is also the reason why you should follow Principle #1 in Chapter One and find help, mentoring, or coaching from someone who is knowledgeable about the goal you seek. They will be able to help you set reasonable goals for your level of expectation. Then you can simply course correct and adjust your goal, striving to lose 50lbs over the next four months instead of two. Let's say the vision in your pillar of health is to have 6-pack abs and feel confident when you take your shirt off at the beach, but you are currently 60lbs overweight. A long-term goal might be to lose 60lbs over the course of one year. To reach this goal, you would need to lose an average of 5 lbs. per month. Therefore, the first short-term goal on the roadmap to hitting the long-term goal would be to lose at least 5lbs the first month.

After you've quantified your goals, the question now becomes, "What must be done on a daily, weekly, or monthly basis in order for me to achieve the short-term goal that's been set?" "How many days a week do I exercise?" "What are the best exercises for me to do?" "How long do my workouts need to be?" If you don't have access to an expert, you can search the answer to this information online or get in action and choose an arbitrary number of days you'll go to the gym per week, what exercises you'll do, etc. A general rule when defining goals toward any pillar, is find an expert in that field! They can help define reasonable goals toward your vision. But also remember, just as important as receiving help toward reaching our goals, is the mandatory action that needs to be taken to achieve them. You can always course correct. As a matter of fact, be prepared to.

Now, regarding our example of the goals we've set for our fitness pillar, another step we would need to implement is a change in diet. If I lacked knowledge regarding this subject, the first thing I'd do, again, is consult a nutritional expert as a start. From there, I'd create steps toward consistently eating healthier by creating long, middle, and short term goals, and figuring out what must be done on a daily, weekly, and monthly basis in order to hit those short-term goals. Examples of questions to ask to figure out what daily, weekly, and monthly activities are needed in order to hit your goal would be, "What foods do I need to eat?" "How often do I eat them?" Once you've figured out what you have to focus on daily, weekly, or monthly, it's simply a matter of scheduling. We are almost done with your roadmap!

TWO NON-NEGOTIABLE PILLARS THAT SOLIDIFY FULFILLMENT

Before we schedule our calendars, let's pause to understand a key point. The pillars, at any given time in your life, will be in order based on the degree of importance each one has at the time, and based on the circumstances in your life. However, there are two pillars that, in order to achieve the highest level of fulfillment, are NON-NEGOTIABLE in terms of priority and should **never** change in level of importance at any stage of your life. They are:

1. Spirituality
2. Family/Relationships

If these two pillars aren't the top two in your life, you will eventually struggle with a decrease in fulfillment. Many people are chasing success because they feel that money, power, prestige, or fame will bring them fulfillment. These things can certainly bring temporary joy and satisfaction, but they will not create ***lasting*** fulfillment. To ensure lasting fulfillment, your spiritual and family/relationship pillars should be prioritized 1st and 2nd respectively. When those two pillars are not prioritized among the others, you run the risk of experiencing problems in your family and marriage. This then spills over into other pillars, resulting in more stress, struggling productivity, and decreased happiness. Both professional and personal peak performance is very important, but should not be practiced at the expense of fulfillment. You should be fulfilled, even if you do not yet have the success you aspire to achieve. Fulfillment shouldn't be dependent on success. A life of fulfillment is one that is independent of any achievement. It is defined by tremendous gratitude and the recognition of past and current blessings we experience. It's the humility to know we aren't in control of everything, and being thankful that God is. It's understanding that our identity is not defined by our title, money, influence, or success, but rather by our character, authenticity, and core values such as love, grace, forgiveness, integrity, and hard work. ***A life of fulfillment is characterized by the gratification experienced by serving others through the pursuit of one's purpose, rather than relying primarily on the achievement of success to sustain happiness.*** And the **only** way this fulfillment is achieved and maintained is by placing God and Family as non-negotiable priorities in your life!

Remember, how we talked about foundation earlier? The two foundational pillars of your life are (1) Your relationship with God, and (2) Your relationship with your spouse/significant other, children, family, and friends. In addition to the fact that it solidifies fulfillment in your life, there are other benefits that come with prioritizing these two pillars in your life. It gives you a system with which to prioritize responsibilities. It also gives you a system with which to say "No" to certain things if they somehow risk compromising the priority of the first two pillars. For example, I attend men's Bible study every 2nd and 4th Wednesday at 7 p.m. It is non-negotiable and does not get moved. Anything that happens on the same time and day as Bible study is an easy "No." I then work my schedule around the daily, weekly, and monthly activities that have been set to help me reach the goals within my first two pillars.

When you do this in the correct order, your journey to success is much easier because you aren't chasing success with the assumption that it will also bring you fulfillment once you achieve it. It will also limit disappointment. Along the journey to successfully achieving your goals, there will be times when you fall short. It happens. If your happiness is primarily dependent on whether you achieve that goal, and you happen to miss the mark, then it could lead to significant disappointment and even depression. However, when you seek to live a grateful, blessed, giving, life of purpose and service (a life of fulfillment), then you don't need success to provide sustained joy, because you already have it! When you seek to live a fulfilled life first, success is like a special, sweet icing on the already robust fulfillment cake!

TIMING AND SWITCHING OF PILLARS

At different times in your life, the order of importance of the pillars will change. There might be a time when your health may change and its priority goes from further down on the list to a higher level of importance, with more time and energy spent on it. For example, if you were to receive a new diagnosis of diabetes or need unexpected surgery, your health pillar would move up in level of importance. Or, if your purpose were really gaining clarity and momentum, unique opportunities to foster growth and the fulfillment of your purpose would take a higher level of importance. One point to make though is that each pillar carries a **major** level of importance, requires regular progress and should have a plan in place for its ultimate vision and destination. Never should someone completely neglect a pillar. People often make statements like, "I just don't have the time to work out or eat healthy, so it's on the back-burner." This "back burner" concept suggests that it's still on the stove staying warm and being given some level of attention. But the reality is, most folks are neglecting that which is on the back burner and should really be saying "It's in the back of the pantry or refrigerator collecting mold!" Every pillar should be on a burner and receiving some level of attention or else it'll be forgotten, and next thing you know, you are trying to figure out what's that smell? By that time, it's molded and rotten and it's too late! None of the pillars, contrary to popular belief, require an extraordinary amount of time to maintain and even advance them.

CREATING A CALENDAR

Now that we have established the importance of the first two pillars and identified the daily, weekly, and monthly activities needed for each pillar, it's time to create a schedule and to-do list of things that must be done in order to achieve your desired result. Each activity **must** be put on the calendar or it doesn't exist and won't take place! Take the time to make the calendar. Start with pillars 1 and 2. For example: If your vision is to have a happier more communicative marriage, as part of your goal to spend more time together, you might want to search for and schedule a yearly marriage retreat, monthly date night, and weekly time together to just talk and catch up and enjoy each other's company. Once those are on the schedule, you then DO THEM and they are NON-NEGOTIABLE! Remember, the spirituality and family pillars are priority amongst all the pillars. Map and schedule those things first. Nothing changes them! You will then do this with every single pillar. Now don't get nervous and think that there will never be time enough for all of this. The more you practice the exercise of going from your vision to actionable steps, you'll notice yourself getting better at it and it will become easier and easier to do. Not all goals that you set for each pillar require something to be done every single day in order to eventually achieve them. Don't get discouraged if some of the steps seem a little more difficult and not as clear at first. Continue practicing. Just like with anything new, there's a bit of a learning curve. But with more practice, the easier and more clear your steps and schedule will become. Write this stuff down. Don't just use your phone or app to do this. Physically write it out. This will help. You'll also see as you schedule these actions, that it really doesn't require a ton of time to give attention to each of your pillars. At first it may take some getting used to, but eventually, you'll be able to juggle all aspects of your life with organization and feel less overwhelmed and stressed.

Think about trying to push a very heavy bolder. It takes the most effort to go from stationary to moving, compared to maintaining its movement once it's already in motion. Once the boulder is moving, it takes much less effort to maintain and keep going. This is the same for the pillars in your life. As you write them down and schedule them out, it may take some effort to get them moving since they have been neglected and stationary for a while. But once you begin moving in the right direction, maintaining the movement with consistent action is much simpler. Also, you can adjust things. Remember, adjustment is expected. The road to your vision can and will change over time. It's ok.

DEFINED GOALS CHAPTER SUMMARY

- Designing the life you desire is like going on a journey, but you must define the end destination first.
- 7 Pillars of Peak Performance
    - These are categories of life that we have a personal responsibility toward maintaining and advancing.
    - The pillars are: 1. Spirituality 2. Marriage/Family/Relationships 3. Purpose/Calling 4. Career 5. Health 6. Wealth 7. Personal Interests
    - In order to practice peak performance and live the best version of ourselves, we must be aware of, maintain, and advance each pillar. No pillar can be neglected!
- Defining Goals
    - Define a vision statement for each pillar
    - Reverse Engineering – Start with your vision of the end result and then work backwards to define what long, middle, and short-term steps/goals you need to accomplish to get there. Quantify and make the goals as specific as possible.
    - Be prepared to adjust and course-correct your roadmap to your goals and vision. A detour on the journey toward your goal, does NOT mean to stop going after it!

- Create a calendar and schedule out the things you need to do daily, weekly, and monthly toward your goals and stick to it!
- 2 Non-Negotiable Pillars that Solidify Fulfillment
- Spirituality
- Marriage/Family/Relationships

Keeping these pillars as top 2 priorities will serve as a foundation toward living a life of lasting fulfillment that isn't dependent primarily on the achievement of success.

- A life of fulfillment is characterized by the gratification experienced by serving others through the pursuit of one's purpose, rather than relying primarily on the achievement of success to sustain happiness.

MORNING HABIT

BENEFITS TO A MORNING HABIT

A morning habit is a routine practiced every morning to get your day started with the appropriate mindset to maximize productivity in your day. It provides structure and organization. It allows you time to think intentionally about what you want to do with your day. Without structure and organization, things can seem very disorganized and cause one to feel lost, stressed, and easily overwhelmed. A great way to describe stress is the physical and emotional manifestations of not feeling in control. A morning routine helps to minimize this because your day now has more order and organization. When done correctly, getting up early to a morning habit also provides you with more energy! I believe that if people practiced a consistent morning habit, they wouldn't rely so heavily on coffee for energy. Rising early increases productivity, because more things can get done early in the morning, rather than staying awake later at night to complete them. It helps minimize mistakes because a review of the "to-do list" of the day allows one to make sure everything gets done without missing anything. It also provides clarity and consistency on daily tasks. It provides a measurable means to determine whether your day was successful. Look at your morning routine like a pilot checklist. Before takeoff, a pilot has a list of things they have to check because if not, the pilot may miss something and place both him/herself and their passengers at risk. You are the pilot to your day and your morning routine is your checklist. Elite-level performers have and consistently practice a morning routine. Like a pilot, they go through their daily morning habit to make sure their day is as smooth, productive, purposeful, and mistake free as possible.

POWER HOUR – 7 CORE COMPONENTS

Your "Power Hour" is one hour every morning, comprised of 7 core components that are dedicated to allow you to safely pilot your day. This means you will need to add an hour to the time it currently takes you to prepare for your day. ***The Power Hour is the most important hour of your day***. It must be non-negotiable! A pilot cannot skip their checklist before taking off on the runway. There is too much at risk if they don't, and skipping your checklist is too risky as well! This is foundational and will be a staple of your life. The Power Hour is a daily practice that sets the foundational roots of your fulfillment and who you desire to become. You will try to negotiate and justify not doing your routine at times, but I'm here to tell you that you are setting yourself up for a future crash if you do that. You'd never negotiate leaving your house in the morning without brushing your teeth or showering, so why would you negotiate the most important hour of your day—one with which every hour after will be more productive, positive, and high-performing!

Power Hour Component #1: Nighttime Preparation

Your morning really begins the night prior. Before going to bed you must prepare physically and mentally for the following day. This means being responsible for your evening by getting a good night's sleep and avoiding reasons to be sluggish and tired, such as being intoxicated or eating right before bed. You should instead prepare for the following day (i.e. putting clothes out, meal prep, setting your alarm, etc.) and rest. A great way to do this is to set a reminder on your phone every night that asks the question, "What do I need to do to prepare for tomorrow?" That should immediately get you in gear to spend the next 5-15 minutes preparing for the next day. Nighttime preparation helps to streamline your morning so you don't have to do this "extra stuff" in sacrifice of your non-negotiable Power Hour. Here are the steps for a successful Nighttime Preparation:

1. Step 1: Set a reminder on your phone - "What do I need to do to prepare for tomorrow?"
    a. You'll do this until it becomes second nature.
2. Step 2: Preparation
    a. Decide what actually needs to be done (i.e. ironing clothes, laying out workout clothes, meal prep).
    b. Set your alarm to allow you one hour to complete your "Power Hour" routine.

    c. Place your alarm in an area where you **must** get up to turn it off.
3. Step 3: Mindset
    a. Go to sleep imagining getting up on time in the morning, full of energy and excited to start your day.

When I started preparing for my day the night before, it was a game changer for me. It shortened the amount of time I needed for my morning. Also, by going to bed with the appropriate mindset of being excited to get up in the morning, I eventually got to a point where my mind and body would automatically wake up just before my alarm sounded, ready to go!

Power Hour Component #2: Relaxation and Focus

Begin practicing simple breathing and relaxation exercises once you are awake and ready to begin your morning. These techniques require spending a brief period of time clearing the mind and focusing on preparing for your day. It clears your brain and allows you to focus on your Power Hour without distraction. It also fully oxygenates your lungs and body, helps to wake you up, and prepares the brain for focusing. Here are the steps for relaxation and focused breathing exercises (time: 1 minute):

Step 1: Find a quiet place where you have little to no distraction (office, closet, etc.) to do your morning routine.

Step 2: Take 5 big, slow, and deep breaths in and fully fill up the lungs.

- Simultaneously think about a characteristic you want to develop as you breathe in (courage, belief, etc.). Pretend as though you are breathing this in!

Step 3: Slowly exhale each deep breathe all the way out.

- Simultaneously think about a trait you want to eliminate (fear, doubt, etc.). Pretend as though you are exhaling this out of you!

Power Hour Component #3: Gratitude

Spend time specifically and intentionally realizing just how blessed you are! This is one of my favorite components of the morning habit! This part of your morning is a major step toward your overall fulfillment. In a world where people are trying their best to "keep up with the Joneses" and worried about what other people think, this really puts things in perspective. You cannot be grateful and envious at the same time. You have to be one or the other, and we spend this time seeing the fullness of our proverbial glass rather than how empty it is. We really get a chance to understand just how truly blessed we are!

This exercise, when done right and consistently, puts life into perspective for us. You don't focus on what you don't have, but are grateful and thankful for the blessings you do have. The reality is this—if you live in America, the richest country in the world, and you make more than $20k/year, you are part of 1% of the richest people in the world! This exercise also helps to realize just how blessed you are and that it can always be worse. Here are the steps for the gratitude component of your Power Hour:

Verbally communicate out loud five things you are currently grateful for about yesterday (Time: ~5 minutes)

1. The list has to be different each day.
2. Become emotionally drawn up and generally grateful for the items on your list. Don't just go through the motions here (and that goes for everything in this program).
3. Optional: Journal it! You can see over time just how much you have to be grateful for.

Gratitude has really allowed me to see just how blessed I am. It has had a tremendous positive influence on my overall fulfillment! I can clearly identify moments in my life where I would not ordinarily have been able to identify the blessings all around me, and now I can. Because of that I have the understanding that I am blessed no matter how successful or unsuccessful I am. I am fulfilled no matter what happens. Therefore, my happiness and joy is not dependent on an event, a title, success at work or in business, or material things since all of these things are very temporary. If your fulfillment is attached to anything outside of your own "blessed being" or is rooted in external circumstances, you won't be able to experience that lasting sustainable fulfillment, that fulfillment of being blessed and happy no matter what. Since consistently doing this exercise, it has allowed me to go after my goals without the added stress of accomplishing it, because I know despite the result of my efforts, I'm blessed already!

Power Hour Component #4: Prayer

This piece is special because it is the part that can affect the original formula for success discussed in Chapter 1. Remember: Results = Our actions + God's input. But the reality is, you will be much more successful at reaching your desired result if it's something that God actually wants you to pursue! So the big question is, how do I know what God wants me to pursue? The good thing is that identifying and applying the gifts, passions, and prior experiences that He's blessed you with is a great start! But the answer to that question comes from prayer!

There are benefits of prayer that you may not have realized. One of the benefits is coming to the understanding that no matter what, no matter how difficult life gets, or the trials you are going through, God always loves you and wants the best for you. This is very reassuring. Another great benefit is that by spending quality time with God and building a relationship, he will convey to you what He wants you to pursue. You will get to know Him and understand what He wants from you. And last but not least, you can take your problems and concerns to him. He's the ultimate listener and the answer to your lack of fulfillment. This is not a book on how to pray or how to build a relationship with God, but here are some simple steps to start:

Spend time with God (time: 15-20min):

- Focus on building a relationship with Him so that you can understand what He wants of you. Spend quiet time with Him and talk to Him about what's on your heart.

- If you are not sure what God wants you to do, continue spending more quality time with Him, giving your undivided attention. He will make clear what He wants of you and you will know more clearly when He's communicating with you.

I can remember before my prayer life was as consistent as it is now, I would always ask, "How can you hear God? What does he sound like? How does he communicate to me?" Just like we've discussed when starting something new or pursuing a goal, one of the first things I did when trying to understand my prayer life and relationship with God, was seek the advice and coaching from someone whose spirituality I admired, had a strong relationship with God, and knew the Bible well. With a combination of his mentorship and my actions, my communication with God became clearer. The good thing is that the more you practice, the more you'll be able to understand Him and know when He is communicating with you. Just like with anything new however, you will initially feel silly or uncomfortable speaking out loud with no one speaking back. My wife and I have been married for almost 15 years and dated for almost 10 years prior to that. I can pick her voice out from a crowd of people talking and she could do the same with my voice. It's because we've spent lots of time with each other and can recognize the unique characteristics in our tones and speech. Your relationship with god is similar. The more you communicate with Him, the more you'll be able to recognize his voice when He speaks. Just keep praying!

Power Hour Component #5: Reading

This is not just "leisure reading," but reading for intentional growth, learning, and expansion of your knowledge. Not to belabor the point, but this reading does a couple of important things: (1) It "waters the soil" to keep the mind positive and avoid negative self-talk. Read books that instruct and inspire, such as personal growth and development books. Some of my favorites include *The Holy Bible*, *Think and Grow Rich* by Napoleon Hill, *As a Man Thinketh* by James Allen, and *The Magic of Thinking Big* by David Schwartz. This time can also be used to read books that relate to a certain pillar you are looking to improve. For example, if you are trying to improve your wealth pillar, read a book on eliminating debt. Or, if trying to improve your marriage, read books on marital advice. (2) This reading also increases the blueprint and knowledge you have to make the best decisions for your life. You should be like a sponge and constantly trying to absorb as much knowledge as you can about life. Like one mentor used to tell me, "You are either green and growing, or ripe and rotten!" A great way to stay "green and growing" is through consistent daily reading. Peak performance requires that you **always** be in the process of reading something! The steps to scheduling reading during your morning Power Hour are:

Read several pages of something empowering daily (~10-15min)

Step 1: Choose a book about something you are looking to grow in or learn more about.

Step 2: Calculate how many pages to read per day to finish the book by a certain time.

- Example: 100pg book; want to finish it in 1 month (30days); 100pgs/30days = 3.3 pages/day

Step 3: Take action and read it every day!

Power Hour Component #6: Daily Planning

This core component is all about creating your to-do list for the day. This to-do list should include the things you need to do on a daily, weekly, and monthly basis to accomplish goals in all pillars of life. This creates structure and order, and ensures that you stay on target toward your long-term goals, assuming corresponding daily activities get done. Creating a to-do list also gives you a measure by which you can determine if you've had a successful day. Here are the steps:

Planning Your "To-Do List" for Today (~5min)

Step 1: Think about your different goals and what needs to be done TODAY to move toward achieving them.

Step 2: Write them down (In phone notes or in a daily planner)

Step 3: Prioritize what MUST be completed today in order of importance or urgency.

Step 4: Set reminders if needed ("Call mom"; "Stop by the bank"; "Conference call")

Step 5: Review and reference your list several times throughout the day to manage your progress.

Power Hour Component #7: Affirmations

This topic was discussed in prior chapters, but as a reminder of some of the benefits, affirmations:

- Plant the input of belief for transformation
- Are imperative for growth, lasting change, and transformation
- Are forms of positive self-talk

Below are ways to include your affirmations into your morning Power Hour:

Affirmations (Time: ~10-20)

Options:

1. Read your affirmations aloud
2. Listen to your affirmations

Reminder: Give the affirmations your undivided attention! Be emotionally attached to them! Envision and feel each affirmation!

What I started noticing when I began consistently listening to my affirmations in the morning is that when I made decisions throughout the day, an affirmation related to a particular decision would suddenly pop into my thoughts. It was almost like a reminder saying, "Remember what you were saying about that this morning?" For example, one of my spiritual affirmations is, "I am a reflection and imitation of God's love in my daily life." Well I started noticing that during circumstances in which I would normally respond in a negative or unkind way, those words would pop in my brain and I was immediately reminded of how I should behave and respond. This would immediately force me to make a better decision than I had been programmed to make in the past. Another example was with one of my health affirmations, which is "I enjoy maintaining a healthy diet and consistent exercise." I found myself, when I would normally make poor choices related to my diet, being reminded to make better choices. Therefore, my decisions were different but congruent with the vision I had for myself.

The things we say to ourselves in the form of affirmations and self-talk is extremely influential on our mind, belief, and results! I am always reminded of a very powerful and true story I read related to self-talk. A woman had been learning about self-talk and began applying the principles to her health to lose weight. She would listen to her self-talk affirmations every morning while preparing for work. Her husband happened to hear her affirmations since he would prepare for his morning at the same time. This went on for several months, the both of them listening every morning to her self-talk affirmations, with the husband just happening to listen since he was in the room at the same time. Well, the woman achieved her weight loss goal, which she'd long been unsuccessful with in the past. And even though the husband hadn't set any weight loss goals, just by being in the environment of the input he received from his wife's self-talk affirmations, he too lost a significant amount of weight! The environment around us and inputs we consciously and subconsciously allow in our minds have great influence on our beliefs, thoughts, and decisions. Self-talk and affirmations work!

Also, keep in mind that your Power Hour may take a little longer to complete when you first begin your practice of it. But just like anything, you will become more efficient with time and consistency. Don't get discouraged. Remember, it's part of the process. It will feel uncomfortable sometimes and there will be times when you don't want to do it, but consistency and resilience will be key to establishing your routine until it becomes second nature!

MORNING HABIT CHAPTER SUMMARY

- Similar to the checklist of a pilot, a morning habit is a **must-do** routine
- The morning habit increases productivity, structure, and organization
- Power Hour
    - 1-hour practiced every morning comprised of 7 core components
        - Nighttime preparation: Prepare for the following day the night prior
        - Relaxation and focus: Complete breathing exercises prior to starting the routine
        - Gratitude: Take time to realize your blessings
        - Prayer: Have a conversation with God
        - Reading: Books to expand your blueprint
        - Daily Planning: Plan a to-do list for your day
        - Affirmations: Listen to your recorded affirmations
    - Practice, practice, practice and you'll get better at your Power Hour!

CONSISTENCY

This is often the one key ingredient missing from those attempting to reach new levels of performance and results. Many people won't maintain the level of consistency in their actions that will create their desired results. Peak professional and personal performance is contingent upon establishing and maintaining consistency. This chapter is dedicated to the understanding and maintenance of a level of consistency that will ensure results.

THE BREAKING POINT

The definition of consistency according to dictionary.com is "The steadfast adherence to the same principles, course, form, etc." In order to see results in a certain goal, it requires just that, steadfast adherence to the activities needed to accomplish the goal. When it comes to consistency of activity and results, there is what I like to refer to as a "breaking point." ***The breaking point is the threshold of which, with enough consistency of a certain action, there is a corresponding result***. And this breaking point can work in both a positive and negative way. For example, in my sports medicine practice I see runners with stress fractures relatively often. These individuals have run so much, and so consistently, that the impact of running has caused their bones to become stressed to the point that it eventually results in a fracture. Stress fractures don't happen with just a few random runs. They happen after a significant amount of accumulated activity in the form of run after run, impact after impact, in a very consistent manner. The bone has a breaking point and it fractures. In a positive way, I see this with strength and conditioning. Individuals who want to increase their strength and muscle mass start off at a certain weight and body composition, slowly increasing the amount they lift. But increasing strength doesn't happen with a few random workouts in the gym. As a matter of fact, despite putting in work in the gym at the beginning of weight training, almost zero tangible results are actually experienced within the first couple weeks. However, with enough accumulated activity in the form of consistent weight training and repetitions in the gym, a breaking point happens, resulting in increased muscle and strength. Unfortunately, all too often, people decide to quit before they reach the breaking point of results. The breaking point varies from person to person and varies from goal to goal. But every goal you pursue has a breaking point. The question is, are you willing to stay consistent enough, for long enough, to experience it?

ACTIVITY ACCUMULATION PRINCIPLE

We make decisions daily, some that benefit us and some that don't. Each decision has a certain level of impact, both in the moment and as a part of a cumulative effect. For example, one of my mentors, a very spiritually sound, financially independent, high performing, and fulfilled individual is known to have read a large number of books and every year reads many more. His secret? He reads 5-10 pages a day. My response to this revelation was, "What? No way!" But let's do the math. We'll split it down the middle and call it 7.5pgs/day. I started looking at several of the books I'd read and many of them averaged a total of approximately 225pgs. 7.5pgs/day multiplied by 30days/month is 225pgs/month, a book a month! That's 12 new books read a year, 60 books read over 5 years and 120 books read in 10 years. A four-year college graduate, depending on the major, reads anywhere between 40-120 books during their college education. Imagine that only 5-10pgs/day could turn into the equivalent of a full four-year degree worth of knowledge over time! The individual days of activity, reading 5-10 pages, is not a lot of pages—not at all. But the accumulation of those pages over time is significant! Small, seemingly insignificant activities accumulated over time, can produce major results!

This activity accumulation principle works for every activity in our lives, both good and bad. ***Small, what appear to be minor, decisions made daily have a large impact on our lives over time.*** No one who's morbidly obese planned on getting that way. It was the activity accumulation of many small, poor dietary decisions made over time. Eating a Big Mac one time is not going to disturb your weight or body composition at all that day. But many Big Macs over time, turn into substantial health and weight changes. It is the same regarding finances. One impulsive purchase is probably okay, but the accumulative effect of multiple consistent impulsive purchases results in a tremendous amount of credit card debt over time. And best believe this is true for every single pillar of our lives!

THE "SINGLE" MINDSET

Achieving consistent results in your life is not about the "homeruns." When highlights for baseball are shown on TV, they show the big glamorous plays or the homeruns and often it's the homerun hitters that get all the fame and stardom. It's big, it's attractive, and it's thrilling. But the reality is that the vast majority of runs scored in baseball start with a simple base hit, a single. No one really glorifies, talks about, or watches the highlights of singles because they are rather boring and uninteresting. But results are all about hitting singles every day. Single, after single, after single, and with enough simple activities (a.k.a. singles) you are sure to consistently score runs. But focusing only on homeruns and big plays will keep you from being consistent. It will cause you to be impatient because the big play isn't happening fast and often enough. It will cause you to lose confidence because you'll be prone to strike out more when all you are focused on is the homerun. It is not uncommon in baseball that the person who has the most strikeouts is also on the leaderboard for homeruns. The cost of striking out so often can have a negative effect on your confidence. But elite-level performance requires an understanding that the cost of focusing primarily on the homerun, the big play, the spectacular move, is too great. You should instead focus and master the single hit. This should not be interpreted as "don't take risks" or don't "swing for the fences." However, this does mean you should wait for the right pitch, at the right time, with the right swing, all of which is relatively rare—then swing for that homerun. In the meantime, concentrate on consistently making contact with the ball. Hit singles and watch how many more runs you score!

By honing in on hitting singles (simple and mundane activities toward your goal) every day, you are able to have more small victories that increase confidence. And by focusing on singles, you will be less impatient because you are consistently seeing results, even if it's not a "homerun." Examples of singles:

1. Spiritually – daily prayer
2. Marriage – monthly date night
3. Career – making the daily sales calls required to hit your goal
4. Health – daily decision to drink water instead of soda which means less calories
5. Wealth – choosing to eat at home instead of going out for dinner which is less expensive

Part of our human nature and one of the things that fulfills us is progress. The "singles" mentality fosters progress. Even if the accomplishment is small, measurable progress and improvement is something that brings us joy and fulfillment. Singles equal progress and therefore adds to our fulfillment!

FOCUS ON TODAY

Often, we get so caught up with what he have to do tomorrow, the next day, and next week that we fail to see the importance of today. One of the biggest things that sabotages consistency is the feeling of being overwhelmed. Being overwhelmed is all self-induced and is the mind's perspective that you have too much on your plate, too much work to do, or too long to go. Feeling overwhelmed happens when people start focusing on just how far away they are from their goal and how much time and effort from where they are now, it's going to take to reach their goal. A way to combat this is to simply focus on today and today alone. When you wake up and go through your Power Hour planning, simply focus on making sure you get today done! If you focus on getting today done, every day, over time results are inevitable. The best way to predict the future is to do work today.

Back when I started taking my health more seriously, I went for a run for the first time in a few years. I had run a few miles before I turned to run back and I looked up and realized just how far away I was from home. I immediately became discouraged when I thought about the distance I had to run to get back. But then I remembered, focus on today. I told myself to just focus on the next step and putting one foot in front of the other. By simply putting my head down and focusing on each step, the daunting task of running such a long distance home seemed to be much more manageable. I rarely picked my head up to look ahead, but focused on the one step I had to take each moment. Before I knew it, I was back home. The same thing happened when I started working on eliminating my medical school debt. Upon completing my degree, I realized that I'd accumulated more than $150,000 of school debt. It seemed overwhelming to try to eliminate this in a short period of time. It was the goal my wife and I had set with our financial team to accomplish this within 10 years. I just remember thinking, let's just focus on what we need to do today with our saving and spending, and it'll happen. Six years later, the debt was eliminated thanks to simply focusing on the day in front of us and not becoming overwhelmed by what tomorrow had to bring.

REASONS WHY CONSISTENCY DOESN'T HAPPEN

Lack of appropriate input and belief

When it comes to accomplishments like running a marathon or successfully running a large business, you'll often hear people say things like, "Oh my goodness, I could NEVER do that!" And that's the absolute truth, particularly if that's what they believe. Henry Ford said it best, "Whether you think you can or think you can't, you're right!" If you don't believe yourself to be disciplined or consistent, you'll never achieve the level of success you desire. The belief in your ability to accomplish your goal MUST come before the desired result does.

Forgetting the "why"

People often lack consistency or even quit altogether if they forget the reason "why" they started in the first place. Or, they quit because their "why" wasn't strong or significant enough in their lives to stay committed to the action when things got tough. By examining or remembering your "why" and connecting it to people, service, and something bigger than yourself, you create a reason to be drawn to do the activities that will get you closer to your goal instead of feeling dragged to achieve it. Your activity is for a higher purpose, for the service of others, and not doing your activities will ultimately be letting someone down. **Your goals must be worth the consistency it takes to achieve them!**

Lack of a routine and structure

Without having a plan in place with which your daily and weekly activities are outlined, consistency is virtually impossible. For example, if you say, "I want to have a happier marriage" but you don't have a plan with which you can consistently do an act of kindness or schedule a date night, then your attempt at a happier marriage is going to be inconsistent. Create a plan consisting of goals that you reverse engineer into daily and weekly activities as outlined in previous chapters.

Not putting it on the schedule

If you don't put something on your schedule, it DOES NOT EXIST! The counter to this statement is that any event you do put on your schedule or calendar DOES exist. Therefore, if you want to be consistent in your actions, start putting them on your schedule and calendar! How many times in the past have you failed to put something on your calendar and forgot to do it simply because you didn't see it on your schedule? Make sure you schedule your consistency.

Lack of accountability

Procrastination and inconsistency not only survives but thrives in isolation! When another person (an accountability partner, coach, mentor, supervisor, etc.) is added to the equation, we often feel more of a need to keep a certain level of integrity and will not want to let them down. It also keeps you true to your word and original goals. Having someone there to hold you to the fire, so to speak, will increase the odds that you will take consistent and immediate action.

PROCRASTINATION HACKS

1. Morning daily planning

    Reviewing your to-do list and planning for your day every morning will provide the structure needed to be consistent in your actions

2. Put it on the calendar

    If you want it to get done, put it on the calendar...period!

3. Pair the action to another consistent behavior

    This is a unique strategy. You can pair an action for which you desire consistency with some other action that you already consistently do! For example, I had a goal that my family would spend more quality time together, so I made a short-term goal to do something together as a family weekly. One of the things we already do as a family is go to church. Therefore, we coupled our church routine with cooking brunch as a family immediately after coming home from service. We all pitch in and then eat at the table together. It's something our whole family looks forward to now and it is all because we found a way to pair the activity with one that was already in place.

4. Minimize distractions

    Consistency requires being proactive by scheduling things, but it also requires the elimination of potential distractions. For example, writing this book required a certain amount of consistency and I knew as long as I tried writing it in front of the television, it would probably not happen. I enjoy watching sports and would have been distracted by the TV, watching instead of writing. Look at the distractions that are in the way of your consistency and begin to either limit or eliminate them.

5. Accountability partner

    Last but not least, an accountability partner is an absolute game changer! I remember when I made the decision to go from being a night owl to a morning person. I'd done some research and read a great book that really persuaded me to be more of an early riser. I then reached out to a friend of mine and told him all the benefits of getting up early in the morning and having a structured morning routine. We then agreed to be each other's accountability partner. For the next 30 days we messaged each other every morning as soon as we woke up and we encouraged each other to get through our 30-day morning challenge. There were some mornings I really didn't want to get up, but then I'd see Jesse's messages saying, "Rise and shine", and I couldn't help but get up. When talking to Jesse, he had the same story as well. Find someone who would be interested in the same or similar transformation you are trying to achieve and go through the journey together. You'll be happy you did!

CONSISTENCY CHAPTER SUMMARY

- Breaking Point – The threshold of which, with enough consistency of a certain action, there is a corresponding result.
    1. Results are **always** beyond the breaking point, but our actions must be consistent enough to get there.
- Activity Accumulation Principle:
    1. Small, seemingly minor decisions, made daily have a large impact in our lives.
    2. Consistent activities accumulate to create drastic results
- The "Single" Mindset
    1. Don't get distracted by the big play and the homeruns
    2. Focus on consistently hitting singles, which is how the vast majority of runs and results are achieved.
- Focus on Today
    1. Don't get discouraged and overwhelmed by focusing on the distance away from your vision.
    2. Focus on simply taking the next step. Focus on "getting today done" to avoid becoming overwhelmed by tomorrow

RESILIENCE

According to dictionary.com, resilience is defined as "the power or ability to return to the original form, position, etc." In other words, it is the ability to rebound, to bounce back. This implies that there is something in opposition, something that caused a change or regression in progress in the first place. Therefore, in order to be resilient and bounce back, a certain amount of grit and fight is required. But this grit and determination is not just to bounce back, but also to do what is necessary to prevent being defeated by the opposition. When it comes to our goals, we are in constant battle of the opposition. What is the opposition you ask? Anything that is preventing you from succeeding. This chapter will outline the resilient mindset required for peak performance and how you can overcome the oppositions to success and fulfillment.

UNDERSTANDING THE OPPOSITION

There is a certain understanding that needs to be established related to your goals and resilience. It is the fact that there will always be opposition to whatever goal you are trying to achieve. Another way to think about it, in relation to sports, is there is always the defense trying to stop you from scoring. In football, the offense's attempt to gain positive yards and eventually score a touchdown, is always being opposed by the defense trying to prevent the team from scoring. If the offense doesn't practice discipline, remain consistent, and fight to gain positive yards, then the opposing defense will surely overcome them. Our lives and goals are no different. The opposing defense to peak performance shows up internally in the form of laziness, negativity, doubt, fear, complacency, and externally in the form of obstacles, setbacks, and challenges. In each of the seven pillars, if we aren't resilient, disciplined, and consistently making the appropriate decisions to reach our goals, then poor performance will take over in the form of: an unhappy marriage, unhealthy lifestyle, lack of retirement and legacy, and overall unfulfillment. We play an active role in making sure our lives don't become defeated by the opposing "defense" which, by the way, NEVER STOPS trying to forcefully stop us from scoring and reaching our goals. Resilience is the insurance that the defense doesn't win!

Life is hard and there is and ALWAYS will be opposition and obstacles. But if we have perspective about this, then it's not a surprise when we do face trials and challenges.

Many of us get discouraged when on the journey toward our goals, we are a faced with obstacle after obstacle, and are surprised when we face new and different challenges over and over. This mindset is the equivalent to driving to a destination, not expecting to have any stop lights, construction, or obstacles that would prevent us from having a straight and easy path to the location. It's similar to fielding a football team with the hopes and expectation that the defense won't field their team, or better yet, will forfeit. If you are aware of and not surprised by the fact that your path will be faced with a defense of opposition and challenges, then it's much easier to go through, because your level of expectation will be different. You can be prepared to face these challenges head-on. It's the difference between watching the weather forecast and bringing an umbrella for a predicted rain shower versus guessing at the weather and being caught in the rain unprepared. Resilience is a key to success, but you have a better likelihood of being resilient when you understand that life and the journey toward your goals will have obstacles. EXPECT THEM! To be forewarned is to be forearmed.

IT TAKES GRIT TO GROW

Once you've come to the understanding that life will have obstacles, curve balls, and challenges, you must then develop an attitude of refusal to stay down. At the core of being resilient is the ability to bounce back, to stand up and prepare to move forward. Obstacles, challenges, mistakes, and struggles all happen for a reason. What's the reason? To help you **GROW!** Start looking at challenges and struggles as simply a way to make you better, to help you improve, to sharpen your skills, and teach you. If you quit because your goal becomes difficult, you can never grow. Success requires growth and learning. Many of us say we want success and even pray for it, but aren't prepared for the tests that we then **must** face in order to grow, learn, and experience the success we desire. ***You CANNOT grow without RESISTANCE!*** When working out in the gym, if you put no weight on the bar, you will never experience growth. The more resistance on the bar, the more you grow! Look at the challenges you face, similar to the weights and resistance in the "gym of life." It's there to promote growth and strength in whatever ways you are being challenged. Don't shy away from it, learn to embrace the struggle. No pain, no gain— literally. The greater the success, the greater the struggles and challenges you can expect. Look at anything you are especially proud of accomplishing and I can almost assure you that the more proud you are of it, the more difficult it was to accomplish. The greater the goal, the greater the grit required to achieve it.

GET UNCOMFORTABLE

The purpose of this book is for you to begin performing at a new level in your life, to perform at a level you have yet to tap into and therefore, experience results you have yet to achieve. In order to do that, this will require you to get uncomfortable. Life has become comfortable for you in areas of either your professional or personal life. At the level of comfort, there is little growth and advancement. However, the level of feeling uncomfortable is where growth, development, and eventual extraordinary results happen. This is true for every pillar (maybe with the exception of personal interests) discussed in this book. If you want to excel in your spiritual life, expect to get uncomfortable. When I really started growing spiritually, I dealt with some major deep seeded issues of guilt, shame, and unforgiveness. It was difficult, but necessary for the spiritual growth I was seeking. If you want to discover and pursue your purpose, expect to get uncomfortable. In my purpose journey, I had to come to grips with the fact that I wasn't yet walking in my purpose. It took time, effort, notes after notes, writing and erasing, and frustration before I found clarity on my purpose. And now that I'm pursuing my purpose there have been even more uncomfortable experiences. It was and is difficult, but necessary and worth it, to achieve a new level of success and fulfillment. ***Expect to be stretched, sometimes to the point that you may not think you can handle it, but know that God won't allow you to experience anything that isn't intended for your overall improvement.*** If you want to improve your health and transform your body, expect to get uncomfortable. When I started training and adjusting my diet to get in the best shape of my life at the age of 37, I was stretched tremendously. There were plenty of workouts where I was more exhausted than I'd ever experienced and wanted to quit, but it was necessary and worth it to hit the next level of fitness I was seeking. And the same goes for your wealth accumulation goals. They will require you to stretch and become uncomfortable as well. After understanding this principle, you may find, as I currently do, that you will constantly seek to push yourself in multiple areas of your life to experience that discomfort. ***Peak performance starts at the level of getting uncomfortable and ends with extraordinary growth, results, and fulfillment!***

SOLUTION-ORIENTED MENTALITY

There is a special mentality that comes with performing at a high level and being resilient. That mentality is positive and focused on solutions instead of dwelling on the problem. When faced with a challenge, obstacle, or mistake, resilience requires that we ask "How" as opposed to "Why." For example, "How can we get this done?" "How can we fix the problem?" "How can we move forward?" These are solution-based questions. This type of mentality focuses on getting back up and seeing mistakes, obstacles, and struggles along the way as mere challenges that only temporarily slow progress toward the achievement of the goal. In contrast, a problem-based mentality is negative and dwells on the problem instead of trying to figure out how to fix it. It sounds like, "Why did this happen to me?" "Why do we have to do this?" "Why is this so hard?" This mentality focuses on complaining about the obstacles stopping the goal from being accomplished. It sees mistakes, struggles, and obstacles along the way as reasons to stop and quit. In order to perform at an elite level, you must have a positive, solution-based mentality, because the reality is, as we established earlier, there will be obstacles and these obstacles are much easier to overcome with the right perspective.

A solution-based mentality also doesn't use circumstances as an excuse for a lack of results. People with a solution-based mentality are not only positive and optimistic, but they are resourceful and find a way to get things done. They have an "I'll figure it out" mentality. This is a HUGE concept to understand for peak performance, because even if you do not know the answer, or have made a mistake, you can always "figure it out"! This is the counter to a perfectionist mentality, which fuels the need for perfection and an insistence on being correct at all times and free of mistakes. The perfectionist mentality halts our progress toward goals because we are avoiding the fear and feeling of being wrong so much that we take little to no action at all. The solution-based mentality says, "Let's give it a try, see how it works, then figure out how to improve it." People with this mentality find a way to "figure it out." Always remember, if you make a mistake, face a challenge, don't know the answer, or happen to move in the opposite direction from your goal, you can always "figure it out" and start again!

STEPS TO RESILIENCE

1. *Belief*

You must increase your belief in 5 areas:

- Ability: Believe in your ability to achieve your goal.
- Possibility: Believe that it's possible for you to achieve it.
- Worthy: Believe that it's worth going after.
- Reality: Believe in the reality of your goal for yourself. You have already achieved it mentally. Now, it's just a matter of time.
- Process: Believe in the process of improvement. No matter where you are now, you can improve

over time. Your belief in these things will fuel your resilience because you have the confidence to go after your goal and you know it's achievable and worth it.

2. *Remember your "why"*
    o Your why is a strong motivating force for achieving your goals and builds the willingness to bounce back up from obstacles along the way.

3. *When challenged, frustrated, or going through a trial ask yourself two questions:*
    o How/What can I learn from this? This will allow you to begin to see obstacles as learning lessons.
    o How can this make me better? This will allow you to begin to see obstacles as opportunities of growth.

4. *Accountability*
    o Resilience sometimes requires us to lean on others when we feel the urge to stop or quit. Having someone there to remind us of our why and encourage us to get back up is important in practicing peak performance.

RESILIENCE CHAPTER SUMMARY

- Resilience – the ability to fight, bounce back, and stand your ground.
- Understanding the Opposition
    1. There is **always** opposition to any goal we are trying to achieve. This **must** be understood and expected.
    2. Life is hard and there will always be obstacles, challenges, and opposition.
    3. To be forewarned is to be forearmed.
- Grit to Grow
    1. Obstacles, challenges, mistakes, and struggles **must** be seen as opportunities to improve, learn, sharpen your skills, and grow.
    2. You cannot grow without resistance!
- Get Uncomfortable
    1. Expect to be stretched and get uncomfortable if you are going to strive for new levels you've never achieved before. This new level will require a new level of discomfort.
    2. God won't allow you to go through anything that's not intended to improve you in some way.
- Solution-Oriented Mentality
    1. Be positive.
    2. In the midst of challenges, focus on solutions and ask questions related to "How" instead of "Why."

3. Don't dwell on the obstacles.
4. Have an "I'll figure it out" mentality.

EPILOGUE

It was an honor and pleasure serving as your success guide along your journey to increased purpose and peak performance. I hope that after this journey, you have a clear vision of becoming the best version of you and believing that it **is** possible to be both successful and fulfilled. This is only the beginning. Remember, this is a guide, so reference this book as often as you need in order to achieve your vision. Don't forget, success and high performance is certainly important, but should not come at the sacrifice of your fulfillment. And if you happened to have achieved the success you desired and it came at the cost of fulfillment, it's okay. You now have a chance to choose fulfillment first moving forward. No matter what, it's time to take ACTION! Take immediate action toward the life you desire and deserve. Master the principles discussed in this book and the steps that follow, and watch both your professional and personal life transform into what you desire: ELITE!

ABOUT THE AUTHOR

Dr. Brad Bellard is a double-boarded Sports Medicine physician and has served as a team physician for multiple professional teams including the NBA Dallas Mavericks. As a non-operative sports medicine specialist, he helps individuals achieve their fitness and lifestyle goals by applying cutting-edge medical procedures to decrease pain and improve function. He serves as a regular guest on the Dallas affiliate of the ESPN 103.3FM radio show, "Inside Sports Medicine," where he educates and informs the public on musculoskeletal injuries and sports medicine topics ranging from diagnosis, treatment, and the business side of medicine.

Dr. Brad is also the CEO of Dr. Brad MD, LLC, where he inspires and coaches professionals on how to maximize performance so they can experience peak levels of professional success and personal fulfillment. He is a compelling keynote speaker, delivering impactful messages on topics including elite performance, purpose, and his personal story of going from ordinary to extraordinary.

To learn more, visit his website at www.drbradmd.com

CREATING DISTINCTIVE BOOKS WITH INTENTIONAL RESULTS

We're a collaborative group of creative masterminds with a mission to produce high-quality books to position you for monumental success in the marketplace.

Our professional team of writers, editors, designers, and marketing strategists work closely together to ensure that every detail of your book is a clear representation of the message in your writing.

Want to know more?
Write to us at info@publishyourgift.com
or call (888) 949-6228

Discover great books, exclusive offers, and more at
www.PublishYourGift.com

Connect with us on social media

@publishyourgift

www.ingramcontent.com/pod-product-compliance
Lightning Source LLC
Chambersburg PA
CBHW052152110526
44591CB00012B/1955